GOD'S TRUTH
for
TROUBLED TIMES

LISA STILWELL

DaySpring

LIVE YOUR FAITH

God's Truth for Troubled Times
Copyright © 2020 by Lisa Stilwell
First Edition, September 2020

Published by:

21154 Highway 16 East
Siloam Springs, AR 72761
dayspring.com

Written by: Lisa Stilwell
Cover Design by: Becca Barnett

Printed in China
Prime: J2435
ISBN: 978-1-64454-814-1

Contents

Are You Prepared? 8

We Must Rest 10

He Is with You 12

His Joy Is Our Strength 14

What, Me? Ask for Help? 16

Diamond-Like Qualities 18

The Solution Is That Simple 20

The Power of His Presence 22

But Lord, I Thought You Said 26

Autopilot or Careful? 28

Conformed to His Image 30

Hold Firm 32

God Has a Purpose 34

Enjoy or In Joy? 36

Golden Bowls of Incense 38

One Day, One Step at a Time 42

Not if, but When 44

Keep Seeking 46

Basic Measures 48

Back to the Starting Line 50

Remain on Solid Ground 52

Trouble Is 54

Before the Love Comes 56

Stand in His Grace 58

Walk in Freedom: Part 1 60

Walk in Freedom: Part 2 62

He Is 64

Let Him In 66

Don't Worry 68

Training Grounds 72

We Will Not Be Shaken 74

Trust in God Alone 76

He Feels Your Touch 78

Safe Delivery 80

Hearing His Voice 82

Lean Back against Jesus 84

Hands Held High 86

Slave or Free? 88

Love More than Win 90

What Now, Lord? 92

He Redeems and Restores 94

He's Before and Behind 98

The Way of Battle Belongs to the Lord: Part 1 100

The Way of Battle Belongs to the Lord: Part 2 102

We Are His Masterpiece 104

When You Pass through Waters 106

No Condemnation in Christ 108

His Way, in His Time 110

Say "Jesus" 112

Prayer—for Everyone 116

When No One's Listening 118

Remember to Refresh 120

The Joy of Victory 122

The Hope of His Calling 126

Why, My Soul, Are You Downcast? 128

Every Day Is Demolition Day 130

Our Loss, His Gain 132

God is With Us—He Is Our Peace (Part 1) 136

God is With Us—He Is Our Peace (Part 2) 138

Acknowledge Him 142

Look for the Helpers 144

Lord, I Want 146

Nothing is Wasted 150

A Beautiful Mourning 152

His Pleasure in Us 154

Above All, Love 156

Give His Way a Chance 158

He Sends 160

Whom Will You Please? 164

We War Not against Flesh and Blood 166

Where is He? 168

Bear with One Another 170

Nothing will Separate Us 174

Why Do You Doubt? 176

Who Wants to Be Blessed? 178

He Fills All Things 180

Fight the Good Fight 184

Are You Ready? 186

Love Him with All Your Heart 188

Foreword

M any years ago, when I was struggling with what to do with my life, I discovered Philippians 4:6–7. Reading those words, I realized that I didn't need to worry about anything, but I did need to pray about everything. As soon as I did so, the peace of God came over me, and I found that God wanted to bless me with His presence. In that troubled time, God's truth brought me peace, guidance, and a solid sense of His presence. And you can have that same experience.

God's Truth for Troubled Times offers encouragement and wisdom from Scripture that teach us how to handle life's challenges and how to live in the center of God's will. Devotions on topics of hope, healing, faith, prayer, and more will touch your heart and even change your life as you read and meditate on God's Word, guided by the inspirational thoughts of Lisa Stilwell.

I have had the privilege of knowing and working with Lisa for the past twenty years. She was a brilliant Senior Editor for the JCountryman gift team for half of that time, and her work improved every project she was assigned.

When I read *God's Truth for Troubled Times*, I was encouraged by her words. My spirit was filled with joy as I meditated on God's Word and her insights. Because of troubled times she has known, Lisa eloquently shares a faith refined by those fires. You'll see how she finds strength in God's Word, and she models how to see God in difficult circumstances. Lisa also challenges you to dig deeper into God's Word to enrich your relationship with your Savior.

This book is a must-read for anyone facing life's challenges and trials. I encourage you to take this book into your prayer life, ask God to reveal what you need to know, and then savor every moment of living in His presence even—or perhaps especially—in troubled times.

Jack Countryman

Introduction

Not long ago, an EF4 tornado ripped through my hometown of Nashville, and I've never felt so close to death in my life. While my neighborhood was unharmed, many others were wiped flat. Nearby homes and businesses were there one minute and completely gone the next. With each news update afterward, I gave continual thanks for God's protection, yet I cried for those who lost their lives and homes. My heart felt bittersweet and sober.

As that first day wore on and I prepared to function without power, I couldn't help but think about all that had happened since I began writing this devotional six weeks earlier. My neighbor was diagnosed with a brain tumor and given six months to live; another received an unexpected bill that would wipe out her savings; the Coronavirus made its entrance and claimed its first death in the US, and immediately people started losing their jobs; news headlines have continued to post chaos and division in our country; now a tornado had cut its deadly path through my hometown and surrounding communities. Dare I wonder what tomorrow will bring?

It used to be that when I heard the words *troubled times*, I'd think of a season in one's life, but lately it's come to mean every day. Every day someone is either in a very trying situation or they're helping someone else who is. The promises of God's presence, power, comfort, and strength—they've never meant more and have only increased the reality of our need for Him and for one another.

It's my hope and prayer that each person who travels this eighty-day journey with me will come to truly believe that, no matter what, God is with them in their own troubling situation. He hasn't gone anywhere, and He is still in control regardless of how our world appears to be falling apart. His Word says we will have trouble, but we have His promises and truth to guide our way and help us through.

The choices are few: we've either got to take Him at His word or not. Hopefully, Lord willing, belief wins, and our love for Him and one another will remain the bond that holds us all together for such a time as this.

Lisa Stilwell

Are You Prepared?

A horse is prepared for the day of battle,
but victory comes from the LORD.

PROVERBS 21:31

It's remarkable, sometimes even stunning, how tumultuous times can either hit us in an instant or sneak up on us over time. There doesn't have to be a rhyme or reason, although oftentimes there is both. And whether or not we understand how or why we find ourselves in turmoil, it's so very comforting to know that, in any case, we aren't alone to fend for ourselves. At the very least, we have three defenses that have proven over centuries to work in favor of certain victory, no matter the circumstance. That's because when we have the Creator of the universe on our side, anything is possible.

Get Prepared: Begin each day quiet before God, praising—yes, praising—Him for His faithfulness and love. Read His Word and meditate on His promises meant just for you. Humble your heart and confess any wrongdoing on your part. Acknowledge your need for His presence in your life. Then clothe yourself with His armor—for protection as well as a readiness for battle.

Be Prepared: Once you get prepared, you're now able to stand strong in your situation and *be*. Be ready to receive God's divine direction either to move forward in offense or to wait in defense (which is often the hardest to do). In either case, you can trust wholeheartedly that He is with you and He is for you.

Go Prepared: When God says "Go," strength and boldness will be your friends. You can set that boundary that needs to be made; have that conversation that needs to happen; forgive that person who consumes your thoughts and leaves you angry; ask for help, even though it goes against your grain.

No matter what you face, getting, being, and going prepared for your battles God's way is the best way to experience His victory in any storm.

Father,

thank You for being not only a loving and faithful friend but my defender, protector, and all-wise leader. I want to go through my battles Your way, because I trust and believe You have only my good in store.

In Jesus' name. Amen.

We Must Rest

He lets me rest in green meadows; he leads me beside peaceful streams. He renews my strength.

PSALM 23:2–3 NLT

If we're all honest with ourselves and one another, it's difficult to find rest in a green meadow when life is turned upside down and in trouble. There simply is no time to stop. People depend on us and work piles wait for us, all while the car maintenance light flashes in front of us. Sitting beside a peaceful stream is often a squeezed-out glimpse of our imagination. Yet restful getaways are vital for connecting with God and with ourselves. Strength is found in being still in the healing balm of His grace.

This doesn't mean we're to run away from responsibilities, it means we're to let the Lord lead us to what He knows will rejuvenate our souls, which is always more of Him. But when we keep pushing and striving, we aren't letting Him lead. He knows better than we know ourselves what will lighten the burdens we carry. He knows how to free us from worry and turn it to wonder—the kind of wonder and trust a child lives in. He knows that when we rest, we refuel with new strength for another day.

Let us all take time to stop, not just in body but in mind and spirit, to turn off the busyness and breathe in His presence, which is calming and good. May we embrace that today is the only day in which we're to live, not in the what-ifs of tomorrow. God isn't a task-master, He is a way maker who parts seas and fills vats to the brim. And He will make a way and lead each of us to the soothing, warm breeze our souls desperately need. It's a promise.

> "Don't worry about your life" (Matthew 6:25).
> "Your heavenly Father already knows all your needs" (Matthew 6:32 NLT)
> "Rest in God alone, my soul" (Psalm 62:5).
> "Peace I leave with you. My peace I give to you" (John 14:27).
> "He leads [us] along the right paths" (Psalm 23:3).

Father,

please do take me away, even if only in mind and spirit. I want to feel the warmth of Your presence and soak it in. I want to take Your lead and push aside anything that isn't necessary for this day. Renew my strength and guard how I use it for all there is to do.

In Jesus' name. Amen.

He Is with You

*Together [two of the disciples] were discussing
everything that had taken place. And while they
were discussing and arguing, Jesus himself came near
and began to walk along with them. But they were
prevented from recognizing Him. Then [Jesus] asked
them, "What is this dispute that you're having with
each other as you are walking?" And they stopped
walking and looked discouraged . . . . They came
near the village where they were going, and . . .
urged Him, "Stay with us, because it's almost
evening, and now the day is almost over."
So He went in to stay with them.*

LUKE 24:14–17, 28–29

One of the hardest things about going through a difficult time is thinking God isn't with you. You can say the words "He is with me" but still not feel it or believe it in your heart, because there's no sign of Him. Well, take heart. You aren't the only one . . . .

Three days after Jesus' death and resurrection, two disciples were walking to Emmaus and arguing over the events of the previous days. They were very discouraged and, I imagine, feeling abandoned. After all, Jesus died. Now what were they going to do? Was anything He told them even true?

In their bewilderment, they came upon another man—Jesus Himself—and invited him to join them as they continued to vent their emotions and try to agree on any sense in the matter. When they all arrived at the village, they invited the man to spend the evening with them and continue the conversation. And he did. Jesus eventually revealed Himself to the men, and as they realized who He was, they also realized He had been with them all along. They didn't feel as though Jesus was with them, but He was. He walked their same road of distress; He participated in the discussion; He stayed with them until they finally realized He was with them as He said He would be.

Friend, He is walking your path with you now. He hears every word that spills from your mouth and feels your heartache or struggle or whatever it is you're going through. It may not feel like it, you may not see Him, but He is there. Now ask Him to stay. Keep engaging Him in the details of your life, and know that He hears and He cares.

Lord Jesus,

even though I don't see You with my eyes,
I believe in my heart that You are with me, and that
You care. Please stay with me throughout this day.
I need You for my every move.

In Your Spirit of truth, I pray. Amen.

His Joy Is Our Strength

Do not grieve, because the joy
of the LORD is your strength.

NEHEMIAH 8:10

Difficult times can bring a downcast state of mind that draws us, and sometimes holds us, captive to sadness and depression we never thought possible. Everyone is susceptible to valleys of darkness and challenged to find the joy they once knew. Grieving is necessary—for a time. God understands grief. He created it so we'd have a way to process the torrents and waves of emotion that stir us so deeply. He also understands that we as humans can only handle so much for so long before strength dissipates and our fight to keep hope alive fades.

Fortunately, in the very depths of pain, God is present, and He brings His joy to share. Like an ice-cold glass of lemonade on a scorching hot mid-summer afternoon, He refreshes the soul. For a time, all the heartache and struggles disappear, and we are carried by His breath of heaven that says, "I love You. Let my joy be Your strength today."

Once the glass is empty, the heat may return, but power is renewed for another day that gets us closer to healing and closer to renewed sight of the King who is over the good times as well as the bad.

Father,

thank You for the compassion and love that You show, especially when I am down. Your joy is like no other— it feeds and restores my soul. Help me not to lean on my own understanding but to trust in You to bring me through this time.

In Jesus' name. Amen.

What, Me? Ask for Help?

*You [Moses] will certainly wear out both yourself
and these people who are with you, because the task
is too heavy for you. You can't do it alone. . . .
In this way you will lighten your load, and they
will bear it with you. If you do this, and God so
directs you, you will be able to endure.*

EXODUS 18:18, 22–23

It's hard for most of us to ask other people for help. Sometimes it's hard to even admit we need help in the first place, let alone ask for it. But we all face times when we can't do life on our own. When we try, exhaustion sets in and isolation leaves us bewildered. Moses had the same problem, and it took his father-in-law to gently point it out and help him realize that if he would only delegate some of his duties, everyone would benefit, not just Moses.

Fortunately, Moses listened and remains a good example that there's absolutely nothing wrong with calling a friend or going to a neighbor (that you don't even know very well) and saying, "I'm having trouble. Could you possibly help me?" In fact, God expects us to. He didn't create us to "hang in there" and simply "get through" life alone. Others actually find their own blessing when we're honest and share a struggle with them. They have them too, and once we're vulnerable enough to expose our weaknesses to one another, there is a communion of love that God instills deep into our very being. When the weight of a burden is carried by two people, there is instant relief, and we have strength for another day.

People need God, but they need other people too. So don't be afraid—or too proud—to be honest and ask for help. Start with God, and trust that He will direct your path toward those who are waiting to extend a blessing your way.

Father,

forgive me for the years I've lived too proud to ask for help. Thank You for gently showing me that I can't do life alone. I need You, and I need my neighbor, and I am grateful for the humility, the richness, and the renewed strength I have found in being on the receiving end at times.

In Your loving arms I abide. Amen.

Diamond-Like Qualities

Blessed is the one who endures trials, because when he has stood the test he will receive the crown of life that God has promised to those who love Him.

JAMES 1:12

What do you get when you take the purest form of transparent carbon, put it 350 feet below the earth's surface in a 2,200° oven, and apply 725,000 pounds of pressure? Diamonds. And because of the process of their formation, they are *adamas,* which is Greek for *indestructible.* Thinking about this reminds me of a line in a song by Hawk Nelson that says God is making diamonds out of us. Honestly, I get so tired of going through trial after trial, I wish God would make me a sapphire instead, don't you?

Seriously, though, the only thing I can think of that is even higher on the scale of indestructability than a diamond is the crown of life. When God's grace is evident and faith is demonstrated in the heat of a trial, our salvation is beautifully clear—not only to ourselves but to unbelievers who are searching for a Savior. The gleam and sparkle a diamond displays is the way God would have our lives appear to a lost world.

Each time you praise God, continue to endure, and reflect His joy in circumstances that are bleak, one more facet of your heavenly design is formed. And the more facets you have, the more you will shine.

So, whatever heat and pressure you are under today, let your diamond qualities prevail. Remain strong and keep His glory in your sights. He is working a masterpiece in you that won't compare to any earthly jewel.

Father,

please forgive my complaining and self-pity when life gets hard. Help me to reflect Your goodness instead. Help me not only to live out the hope I have in You, but also to share my hope with others who are struggling as well.

To You be all the glory. Amen.

The Solution Is That Simple

Don't let your heart be troubled.

JOHN 14:1

I don't know about you, but sometimes I feel anxious or unsettled inside without even knowing what it is I am feeling anxious about. It's very frustrating. All I want to do is try and figure out what the problem is so I can deal with it and get back to a state of peace again. Can you identify?

Sometimes I read the Bible to find a verse that will point to what the problem is. I'll pray and be silent before God to get the reason and the help I need from Him. Oftentimes taking these steps work, but sometimes I can spend an hour doing both and nothing will have changed—I still feel anxious. The last time this happened, I was just about to close my Bible when my eyes caught this verse in John: "Don't let your heart be troubled." It was as though the words jumped right off the page and into my soul. I did a double-take and read them again. They didn't say why or provide a reason for my anxiety, they just said not to be that way. So, I took Jesus at His word and decided not to be troubled, simply because He said not to be. And peace returned.

God isn't complicated, but we often make Him that way. Even when we do know what makes us anxious, the solution is still the same: don't let your heart be troubled. Sometimes a modest, unpretentious decision to do what

God says to do, without having to have a long, analytical explanation for doing it, is all we need. It truly is enough.

What about you? Will you meekly and humbly choose not to let your heart be troubled today? His peace that passes all understanding is waiting to fill you to overflowing. Now let it.

Lord,

thank You for Your patience while I run in circles to resolve a problem. Thank You for the power and life Your Word has to offer. And thank You for putting Your peace into every anxious thought I can imagine.

I adore You. Amen.

The Power of His Presence

We [Paul and Timothy] were completely overwhelmed—
beyond our strength—so that we even despaired
of life itself. Indeed, we felt that we had received
the sentence of death, so that we would not trust in
ourselves but in God who raises the dead.

II Corinthians 1:8–9

Death sentence. Those words instantly convey an end without hope. When sentenced to death, you're alive now, but death is ahead, and there is no escaping—at least not with human logic or strength.

Sometimes, like Paul and Timothy's experience, life can be so overwhelming, it can feel like a death sentence. We are brought to the end of ourselves—there is nothing left we can do or give. Every ounce of life as we've known it is gone. This state of mind sounds so ominous and grave. But it depends on perspective—the perspective Paul and Timothy had.

They saw their death sentence as a reference point for where God would pick up where they left off. If He wanted to take them to their heavenly home, eternal life awaited. If He chose to orchestrate their circumstances to make a way out, new life on a new path awaited. Either way, no death can withstand the power of His presence; no end is final when it's met with God's resurrecting ability. When looked at that way, the meaning of death changes to new life every time.

What in your life feels like a death sentence? Will you agree to its end and let the God of all comfort begin afresh? Will you trust in His power and rest in His plan? He loves you and has only your good—and His glory—in mind. You can rest in that and never succumb to the power of death again.

Father,

thank You for a new way of looking at loss in my life. Thank You for bringing me to the point of knowing that, no matter how overwhelming life can be, You are working life into every aspect for my good. I want to rest in You today and just be in Your life-giving presence.

All glory to You. Amen.

*If you're ever tempted
to avoid the unattractive
path God has planned,
turn to Jesus on
the cross. See Him
as a reminder that
priceless treasures
are in broken vessels.*

CHRIS TIEGREEN

But Lord, I Thought You Said

Pharaoh said to Joseph, "I am Pharaoh and no one will be able to raise his hand or foot in all the land of Egypt without your permission."

The story of Joseph is no less than amazing. When he was seventeen, God showed him his future in a dream where Joseph's father, mother, and eleven older brothers would bow down to him (vv. 7, 9). But what God didn't show him was the route he'd take before he got to his royal status. His brothers threw him in a pit, sold him into slavery, and faked his death to their father. From slavery, he was falsely accused of making advances toward a high official's wife and thrown into prison for twelve years. It wasn't until his thirties that he was released and finally rose to second in command only to Pharaoh.

Can you relate? Has God placed a dream or a calling in your heart, maybe even led you to pull up roots and move to a new city or job or ministry, only to feel as though you've made the biggest mistake in your life? "But Lord, I thought You said to do this . . . I thought You opened these doors for me to walk through . . . I thought I had Your blessing in this, so why aren't things turning out?"

These are times to remember that doing and being in God's will doesn't equate to smooth and easy times. In fact, it's usually the exact opposite. Not only is there a spiritual battle that rages where our enemy doesn't want us to succeed,

26

God is always working to purge, purify, refine, and make whole our relationship with Him. New ministries and doing His will aren't necessarily the focal point of His desires. He wants you, me, all of us to become all He knows we can be, and it's in the trials and hurdles where we not only rise to more than we ever thought possible, but also to where we create new stages for highlighting His glory.

Father,

forgive me to second-guessing You and Your plan for me. Forgive me for wanting to give up so easily at times. Help me to see Your hand no matter how difficult my situation and know that You are working things out for my good and for Your glory.

In Jesus' name. Amen.

Autopilot or Careful?

*Carefully observe the commands of the Lᴏʀᴅ
your God, the decrees and statutes he has commanded
you. . . . Carefully follow every command I am giving
you today, so that you may live and increase,
and may enter and take possession of the land
the Lᴏʀᴅ swore to your fathers.*

Dᴇᴜᴛᴇʀᴏɴᴏᴍ(6:17, 8:1

Have you ever driven somewhere only to realize that, once you arrived, you don't even remember the drive? Your mind drifted into a different train of thought without even realizing it, and you drove on autopilot. When this happens, it's a relief any of us get to where we're going safely. Does this sound familiar?

"Honestly, officer, I wasn't trying to speed, I just wasn't paying close attention to the speed limit."

"You mean you didn't see the flashing yellow lights and the SCHOOL ZONE sign hanging from above?!"

Well, sometimes we can go through our Christian-living motions much the same way. We get so distracted by our empty bank accounts, a loved one who is ill, or a child who is wayward, and we go through our day without intentionally thinking about God and what He would have us do. We say we'll pray for someone, but we're too preoccupied. We see the homeless man asking for a donation and look beyond. We flash our selfie smiles out to others while our hearts are really turned inward on our pain or frustration about something else.

God knew we'd have this problem, and that's why He stated twice, fairly close together, to "carefully" observe His commands. When we're careful, we're intentional—we're full of care. When we're careful, we hear His voice above all the other noise. When we're careful, the depths of our hearts are focused on others, not just the surface of our outward faces. And when we're careful, we have a brighter view of hope in our struggles.

In the midst of our problems, let's be mindful of the Lord and His ways, so that we may live and increase to the fullest, because that's what He says will happen when we do, and He is faithful to do what He says.

Lord,

the next time I start to go on autopilot, please let me know. Don't let my challenges take the spotlight of my mind rather than You. I don't want to miss all the good You have planned, not just for me, but for others as well.

In Your sweet name. Amen.

Conformed to His Image

[God] knew those who would be His one day,
and He chose them beforehand to be
conformed to the image of His Son.

ROMANS 8:29 THE VOICE

Isn't it a wonder that each of us was chosen by God? That means both you and I—we were chosen. And He explicitly wants us to be conformed to the image of His Son, Jesus. When I think of Jesus's image, I first think of all that is lovely, compassionate, patient, powerful, servant-minded, forgiving, and truly caring about others. But on second thought, Christ's image also consists of so much more. Like pain. And waiting. And temptation . . . Then there is hunger, rejection, unbelief, even suffering . . . to the point of death. When we compare that part of His image to the trials we are in, who are we to think we're above the same? And how does this realization make a difference in our lives and help us now?

Well, I look at the fact that Jesus didn't react to anything as though it was a surprise. No, instead of reacting in fear, He responded in faith to each and every situation. Responding is where He truly longs for us to conform. He wants us to remain in faith that He has a plan that He's working out for our good and His glory—no matter what we are facing.

Can you imagine what your life would be like if you were able to respond in faith to your tribulation as Jesus did?

Or what the church would look like if it responded in faith to the verbal mudslinging and toxic headlines we're so often bombarded with? None of the valleys we find ourselves in are a surprise to God. And how we are to respond to them isn't a secret—it's a choice. Through the power and example we have in Jesus, we can conform. The question is, will we?

Father,

I am both honored and humbled to be in Your family. The next time I'm tempted to react with panic in my heart, please remind me that I have a choice to respond in the faith I have in You. You are a faithful God, and I long to be in the fullness of Your grace in any storm I face.

In Your Son's precious name. Amen.

Hold Firm

*Do everything without grumbling and arguing,
so that you may be blameless and pure, children of
God who are faultless in a crooked and perverted
generation, among whom you shine like stars in the
world, by holding firm to the word of life.*

PHILIPPIANS 2:14–16

Our culture today lends itself to so much arguing and fighting. Headlines report of this battle and that offense. Yet, when reading this verse, it's evident that "arguing and fighting" in a "crooked and perverted generation" is nothing new under the sun. There is as much fighting in our world today as there was thousands of years ago. There weren't as many people and there was no social media or television to report every incident 24/7, but the fighting was still there.

Thank goodness God has given us all an anchor— His Word—to hold firm to. It's an anchor that's lasted up through time and something we can grasp at any given time to receive instant relief and assurance of mind. But anchoring doesn't mean reading a verse, say, about forgiveness and trying to forgive. It means holding on to the process day after day—sometimes year after year—the way a rock climber holds on to any nook and cranny he or she can find while climbing up a cliff. Sometimes that's what the process feels like. When adrenaline skyrockets in response to hurtful words or deceitful acts, the quickest and most effective way to land on peaceful ground is to land in the middle of a promise—His promise—of love, of justice, of faithfulness, and of truth.

It's both rare and refreshing to hear about acts of compassion and simple kindness, turning what could have been a story with a negative outcome into one that ends in peace and unity. I suppose that's why, when we do hear about them, they shine like stars in the backdrop of a very large and black sky.

Let us all be stars! When life of any kind is threatened—whether in a conversation or a media post or a hateful action—let us hold on to God's light and love rather than let the light of life go out.

Father,

please diminish the noise around me that breeds chaos, and let Your words of truth be my stronghold today. Lead me to Your promises and help me commit and apply them to my daily life. Help me to be a light of hope and love to a world that needs a Savior.

In Your name I pray. Amen.

God Has a Purpose

*I, John, your brother and companion in the tribulation
and kingdom and patient endurance* which are *in
Jesus, was on the island called Patmos, [exiled there]
because of [my preaching of] the word of God
[regarding eternal salvation] and the
testimony of Jesus* Christ.

REVELATION 1:9 AMP

John spent his entire life in service to God, yet there he was toward the end of it, exiled on an island because of Christian persecution. At first glance, it would be easy to rush to judgment and ask God why He would allow such a sentence on someone who spent his entire life devoted to Him. It can be asked of many of us today who love and serve the Lord our whole lives but whose circumstances take such a turn, the good life as we've known it is gone. Sickness, debilitation, bankruptcy, death—life can take detours we don't expect, and through all the twists and turns, we can find ourselves alone in a strange and isolated space.

But God has a purpose any time life comes to a halt and surroundings look foreign. In John's case, his exile not only had a purpose, it was orchestrated. God wanted John alone without any distractions so he could process the visions God gave in order to write Revelation—the grand finale of the Bible! It was in exile, or prison, where Paul had the time and space to write numerous books in the New Testament for us to know more about God and the love and grace that is ours through Him. And, friend, if your life is in a place that is nothing like you had planned, God has a purpose in it too. It can actually be the beginning of one of the richest and most prosperous times you've ever experienced. God will use the time He has alone with you to reshape and use you in ways you never thought possible, if you'll let Him.

So, while being in exile can be very hard, sometimes it's what it takes for God to get our full attention and do with us as He will—for our good and for His glory. It's one way for Him to reveal who He is and use our life stories to bless others and show them the way toward Him.

Father,

forgive me the times I've complained about where You have me in life. I forget that You are always working a bigger picture, a greater plan than what I see. I believe there is purpose in everything You allow in my life, so I will rest in that.

All glory to You. Amen.

Enjoy or In Joy?

You have put more joy in my heart than they have when their grain and new wine abound.

PSALM 4:7

It's difficult to look at social media posts made by people who are living the life you wish you had, especially when you're going through a hard time. It's the breeding ground for comparison that opens a door for the enemy to rush in and convince us we don't have a good life compared to others.

Another friend is getting married, and I'm still single. He just got promoted, and I got passed over—again. That couple is having another baby, and our nursery is still empty. They're on another vacation cruise, and I'm working two jobs.

Comparing our lives to someone else's is a surefire way to fall into the pit of pity, and the climb out is long and arduous at best. When we fall into that deep dark state, it's virtually impossible to enjoy life, at least in the way the world says we are to enjoy it. But, praise God, the world's way is not the way to experience joy. I say this with full conviction because, while one may struggle to enjoy life, we can always live in joy—in His joy—and there is no greater and lasting satisfaction. We can, in joy, experience the deepest and widest love and assurance we ever thought possible. In His joy, God flings His loving arms around us and carries our burdens, lifts our spirits, assures us of His presence (even if He has to do it over and over again), and instills in us a peace that nothing on this earth can give.

We can live it up, party all we want, vacation and indulge, and not even come close to the satisfaction of living in joy and complete union with Christ.

It's in His joy where we release all anxieties, because they aren't allowed near His throne. The weight and worries that call for our attention have no voice because joy rings louder. So the next time you start to compare and struggle to enjoy your life, choose to walk in joy—the kind that lasts forever.

Father,

help me not to look at others' lives and, instead, look at You. I want Your joy—the joy of Christ— the only joy that lasts.

Amen.

Golden Bowls of Incense

When [the Lamb] took the scroll, the four living creatures and the twenty-four elders fell down before [Him]. Each one had a harp and golden bowls filled with incense, which are the prayers of the saints.

Revelation 5:8

Prayer is an absolute divine gift from God. We can do it at any given moment—no place or appointment needed. We have complete freedom to turn to Him and talk whenever we want, about whatever we want. Nothing is off limits. There is no time limit. There is no wrong way to do it.

God loves our prayers, especially when we're real and honest from the core of our hearts. And sometimes—the times we have no words . . . when all we have are tears and silence—He hears those too. They are all an incense—a pleasing aroma—He keeps in golden bowls.

Paul says in I Thessalonians 5:17 to "Pray without ceasing" (esv). Other versions of the Bible say, "Pray constantly" (csb), "Pray continually" (ceb), "Never stop praying" (nlt), and my favorite, "Make your life a prayer" (tpt). We are to be always in the spirit of prayer and communion with God. He cares about every detail we try to process in our busy minds for guidance, answers, comfort, purpose, even for simply knowing we are not alone, because we aren't.

When we pray, we offer our powerless state into His all-powerful hands, and He gladly receives it. We also bless

Him with our praise and thanksgiving, because there is much to be thankful for, even in troubled times.

Do you need rescuing? Pray for a life rope.
Do you need provision? Pray for it in abundance.
Do you need a hug? Pray for the comfort of His love to envelop you.

He will answer them all. He is waiting to hear from you.

Father,

*thank You for the gift of prayer. I call out to You
and lay my life before You, because I need Your help.
Please hear my cries; please lift my burdens; please
hear my praise for Your sweet love toward me.
I love You and thank You for rest and assurance.*

There is no one like You. Amen.

Prayer is the key to heaven, and faith is the hand that turns it.

THOMAS WATSON

One Day, One Step at a Time

*Don't be anxious about tomorrow. God will take care
of your tomorrow too. Live one day at a time.*

MATTHEW 6:34 TLB

O ne morning I received a very large and unexpected bill
that completely rocked my world. I quickly sat down,
melted down, and broke down into tears. I imagine most
of you reading this can identify. We all come to times and
circumstances when the words *don't be anxious* don't regis-
ter very well—it seems impossible not to be. Personally, I
don't rush into panic mode often or easily, but even I have
my moments. And even though I'm very familiar with Jesus'
words saying not to be anxious about tomorrow, what do
you do when a bill you can't pay or a need you can't fulfill is
in a not-so-distant tomorrow?

Well, the answer plainly lies in the words that follow:
Live one day at a time. Even better, live one step at a time.
I like the way Thomas Carlyle puts it: "Our main business
is not to see what lies dimly at a distance, but to do what
lies clearly at hand." Tomorrow is a distance just far enough
away that we can't see between where we are now and where
we'll be then. Today is the day we are to keep our steps, keep
our thoughts, keep our actions, and keep our belief in God,
with the hope and faith that what we do today will benefit
into the next. Then, if anything more is needed for tomorrow, God promises to provide it (see Isaiah 58:11).

So, what does living in today mean? It means making a list of what you do have control over and committing to doing it. Then making a list of what you don't have control over and entrusting it to the One who does. That "entrusting" part may have to be done numerous times a day, but I don't think God minds. He just wants us to keep trying and keep believing one day at a time.

Lord,

I trust You, and I entrust all that I can't control to Your loving hands. You make a way when there is no way, and I believe You will do this for me now. I love You and thank You for peace that comes when I rest and trust in You.

In the power of Your name I pray.
Amen.

Not if, but When

*When you fast, put oil on your head and wash your
face, so that your fasting isn't obvious to others but
to your Father who is in secret. And your Father
who sees in secret will reward you.*

MATTHEW 6:17–18

Sometimes, when we find ourselves in the middle of a
battle, one of the best ways to fight through it is to
spiritually decontaminate and renew our minds so that all
we see is the hope of glory. One way to do this is by fasting—
an act of worship that brings a cleansing of the heart, a
clearer perspective, a better ability to hear from God, and a
solid foundation for receiving His favor. In the verse above,
Jesus doesn't suggest fasting. He doesn't even say *if* you fast.
He says "When you fast . . ." He fasted for forty days and
nights while dealing with temptation from Satan, and He
was the victor for it. When we fast, we too can experience
the same breakthroughs for ourselves, so why wouldn't we?

Hunger in the body translates into hunger for God—
for spiritual nourishment, sustenance, clarity, and strength.
"Jehoshaphat . . . proclaimed a fast for all Judah, who
gathered to seek the LORD" (II Chronicles 20:3–4); "Esther
[replied] to Mordecai: 'Go and assemble all the Jews who
can be found in Susa and fast for me'" (Esther 4:15–16); "I,
Daniel, was mourning for three full weeks. I didn't eat any
rich food, no meat or wine entered my mouth, and I didn't
put any oil on my body until the three weeks were over"

(Daniel 10:2–3). These are just a few instances in the Bible when a fast was held during times of calamity and hardship.

God knew we would have troubled times and that they'd get our focus off His splendor and onto our problems. But out of His goodness, He made a way to clear out all the muck in our minds to hear His voice, to walk in His power, and to remain in His peace. What a wonderful Savior we serve.

Jesus,

when times are hard, it's difficult to see clearly and keep my thoughts captive to You. Give me the stamina and courage to do with less today to gain more of You in the days ahead. Anything to bring me closer to You.

In Your great name. Amen.

Keep Seeking

But Mary stood.

JOHN 20:11

Mary Magdalene stood outside the tomb where Jesus lay. Engulfed in a wave of grief after watching His torture, crucifixion, and death, she cried. This is striking because I think any one of us would have been on the ground curled up in a fetal position. I would have been delirious, faint-hearted, and probably incoherent from the sobbing and wailing and grief . . . but Mary stood. It's as though God's grace and mercy guarded her heart and planted her feet on solid ground because He knew the story didn't end there. Victory was in her presence, she just hadn't seen it yet. He held her up until she saw for herself that Jesus was alive.

While Mary was standing, she was also seeking. She stooped and looked into the tomb. Or perhaps she was standing because she was seeking. Her desire to be with Jesus didn't wane—her hope light was still burning. She didn't let the grim events leading up to that morning stop her from trying to be with her Savior.

Friend, I don't know what trouble you face or what has threatened to rob you of hope for your future, but I do know that your story hasn't ended. When death and doubt seem to be all around, God, in His resurrecting power, responds to the seeking heart the way He did Mary's. Through the power you have in Christ, your feet are firmly planted so that no matter the ferocity of the storm, victory is yours long before the storm ends. It may not appear that way now, but faith and hope begin afresh with each new day. So keep looking. Keep standing. Keep believing in the One who brings the victory for us. He is with you.

Father,

thank You for the testimony of Mary and her faith to remain standing in the midst of incredible grief. I ask that You help me to do the same. Give me the strength to keep searching for You in the midst of difficulty. Help me to live in victory today and hold on to hope for tomorrow.

All praise and glory to God in the highest. Amen.

Basic Measures

*[Elijah] said, "I have had enough! L*ORD*, take my life . . . ." Then he lay down and slept under the broom tree. Suddenly, an angel touched him [and] told him, "Get up and eat." Then he looked, and there at his head was a loaf of bread baked over hot stones, and a jug of water. So he ate and drank and lay down again. Then the angel . . . touched him. He said, "Get up and eat, or the journey will be too much for you." So he got up, ate, and drank. Then on the strength from that food, he walked forty days and forty nights to Horeb, the mountain of God. He entered a cave there and spent the night.*

I KINGS 19:4–9

It's interesting how in one season of life we are able to stand strong in the battles we face, and in another season live in absolute fear and worry—to the point of complete exhaustion. When that happens, it's hard to know how to keep fighting when all we want to do is stay under the covers and hide from the tragedy of what's happening around us. Elijah had the same experience. He wanted to die rather than face Jezebel and her desire to kill him. He quickly descended from a mountaintop victory into a marathon race of fear.

Elijah cried out to God without holding back; he had literally given up. And God probably thought, *It's about time, Elijah. I've been waiting for you to give up so I can begin to work.* Giving up and coming to the end of ourselves is oftentimes what must happen before God will enter in and restore us for what lies ahead. And oftentimes that means resorting to the most basic measures: eating right and getting the rest we need. These are hard to do when there is so much to do. Difficult situations don't care that our families need us and deadlines loom over us. But nourishment and rest are vital for renewed strength and a clearer perspective. Everything looks better after a hot meal and a good night's sleep—or two, or three.

Once Elijah ate and rested, it was then that he encountered the Lord. It was then that he received the instructions and encouragement he needed for the next leg of his journey. And it was then that he was able to stand back up with newfound confidence and hope for another day.

Father,

help me to take the time I need to eat and rest—truly rest. Help me to clear my schedule and stop. Bless me with sleep so that when I wake, my energy is restored and my mind is clear. I want to hear Your voice.

In Jesus' name. Amen.

Back to the Starting Line

They didn't trust *Me. They didn't* obey *My voice.*
They refused to listen *to Me. Instead they*
followed the plans of their own stubborn hearts.
Each step was a step backward, not forward.

JEREMIAH 7:24 THE VOICE, emphasis added

If you are a parent, you can probably think of at least a few times you warned your son or daughter not to do something. But nooo, they thought their way made more sense and then walked right into a bad situation. It's very hard to watch and even harder not to be able to stop them because you know that whatever it is they're about to do is going to hurt—a lot. Sometimes the hurt is immediate; other times it comes back to bite them years later. If only they had listened . . .

Yet we, as adults, do the same thing—maybe not with an earthly parent, but often with our heavenly One. We have God's Word that provides answers for handling every problem we face. We have the gift of prayer where we can talk to Him directly for His help and guidance and assurance. We can fast and pray for hearing God's voice and gaining spiritual perspective. And yet we continually resort to our own logic, our own plans, our trust in ourselves rather than trust in Him. God calls this going backward, not forward. Why, oh why do we do this?

The words *trust, obey,* and *listen* are three actions that equate to forward motion, which is what we all want for our lives, isn't it? But sometimes it's three steps forward, two steps backward. So, when that happens, it's okay to circle right back around to the starting line to begin afresh. Thank goodness the Lord doesn't scold or balk. He may be grieved over the pain we bring on ourselves, but His mercies are new every morning. We serve a loving and patient God.

Father,

forgive me the times I've turned to You last and not first. Forgive me for not trusting You for the answers and provision I so desperately need. Thank You for Your grace and especially Your patience as I constantly have to make my way back to You. You were right to refer to me, to us, to the human race as sheep! But You are so good to continually rein us back into Your safe shelter.

You are so good. Amen.

Remain on Solid Ground

*Our eyes are on the LORD our
God until He shows us favor.*

PSALM 123:2

Not long ago I was running through my neighborhood
and saw what looked like a sinkhole in the middle of
a field. I decided to get closer to see it up close—I'd only
seen pictures of sinkholes in news headlines and not in real
life. When I got to its edge, I had no words! It was maybe
twenty-five feet wide and about twenty-five feet deep—big
enough for a car to fit in. What had been solid ground
for years dropped down into the earth in an instant, just
like that.

I took a picture of it and managed to include my shad-
ow standing on the edge to give a good perspective of just
how big the hole was in relation to my small frame. Looking
at it made me think of how some of the problems we face
can feel as big and deep as that hole looked, and we have
no words. It's no wonder we have meltdowns and panic attacks—having to face a problem or fill a need that is ten,
twenty times our size is overwhelming. It's easy to understand why some people fall apart in the process.

But I also thought about Jesus' parable in Matthew
about how everyone who hears His words and acts on them
is like a sensible man who built his house on a rock. The
rain fell, rivers rose, winds blew and pounded the house, yet
it didn't collapse, because its foundation—the man's hope—

was in Jesus, not on the things of this world (see Matthew 7:24–25).

We will all face adverse conditions. There will be times when impossible odds come against us. You might be facing some odds right now. But when we put our hope in Christ, we can stand firm and not lose it. We can boldly claim the promise that "I can do everything God asks me to with the help of Christ who gives me the strength and power" (Philippians 4:13 TLB).

So whatever enormous problem you're looking into, look up to the One who is greater instead. He is much bigger, and He promises to guide your way and be "a very present help in trouble" (Psalm 46:1 ESV). Stand firm on solid ground by keeping your eyes on Him.

Lord,

with so many uncertainties in life, I look to You, Your Word, and Your help every day. You are my strong Rock, and I stand in confidence of Your presence and love.

In Jesus' name. Amen.

Trouble Is . . .

*The righteous cry out, and the LORD hears,
and rescues them from all their troubles.*

PSALM 34:17

Trouble is . . . It's in each day and seems to be everywhere. It's in the car that won't start and the divorce papers waiting to be signed. It's in a child's rebellion and the basement that's flooded. It's in the flames of a house fire and a virus spreading worldwide. Jesus said we're to expect trouble, and that is the truth. We can be the victims or the cause, and no race, demographic, age, or social status can escape it. We will have trouble—we're in it now.

Jesus also said He'd rescue us, and that is the truth. We are not left alone to fight for a better day. The Lord hears when we call His name. He hears every word that we cry out and plead to Him for help. No valley is too deep, no pain is too great that His Spirit won't go to heal and to comfort, to save and to restore. And when the pain is so great it chokes back our words, He hears the silent cries of our souls and rushes in to hold us up.

Jesus is the name to call on for deliverance—through not just some, but all trouble. He is the name to call for the strength to endure. He is the name to call for the faith to keep going. He is the name to cry out for fanning the flame of hope to keep burning.

So whatever trouble you're in today, whatever unknown trouble is yet to happen, whatever trouble you see approaching on the horizon, cry out to Jesus! He hears and He cares. He will rescue you.

Lord,

thank You for rescuing me over and over and over again. Thank You for the times I haven't cried out, yet You've rushed to me anyway.

I love You. Amen.

Before the Love Comes

*Love your enemies and pray
for those who persecute you.*

MATTHEW 5:44

If you're going through a rough time, there's a good chance other people are involved. There are probably a few names that, when mentioned by someone else, even in passing, make your spirit quicken and your lips purse so you don't say something regrettable. We all have a delicate path to walk toward loving and praying for our enemies. They've hurt and offended and deceived us or someone we care about. Loving and praying for them is not what we want to hear or do.

This brings to mind King David's prayer for God's enemies in Psalm 83. He writes: "Deal with [Your enemies] as You did with Midian . . . . They became manure for the ground. . . . Make them . . . like straw before the wind . . . and terrify them with Your storm" (vv. 9–10, 13, 15)! David didn't hold back his feelings *at all*, at least not before he eventually moved into lament a few psalms later. He had to vent and confess his own vengeful thoughts before he could calm down and get back to the goodness of God and His grace. The beauty is, David didn't focus his anger on the enemy, he released it to God's listening ear—and he left the consequences to Him. When we do the same, we begin to restore.

David's relationship with God was so close, he felt safe to be honest in his struggle, and we can too. Sometimes, in order to get to the love and prayer part for our enemies, we have to blast off the anger and hurt and betrayal to the One who understands better than anyone. As we do, the forgiveness He has shown us can flow into our forgiveness toward them. And love wins.

Lord,

thank You that I can be real with You. Thank You for being a safe place to release my true feelings and to know that You hear and care. Help me in my journey toward loving and praying for my enemies. Keep bringing the point home that Your ways of dealing with troubling times carry eternal consequences, not only for me but for others as well.

In Jesus' great name. Amen.

Stand in His Grace

This is the true grace of God. Take your stand in it!
I PETER 5:12 HCSB

If anyone understood the death one feels when separated from God, it was Peter. He denied knowing Jesus not once but three times, and as a rooster crowed, Peter recalled Jesus' words to him earlier, "'Before the rooster crows, you will deny Me three times . . .' And [Peter] went outside and wept bitterly" (Matthew 26:75). I can understand the depth of despair he felt, because, while I haven't denied knowing Jesus, I have denied Him personally through rebellious acts. It's a dark, frightening, and humiliating state to be in.

The most difficult part to comprehend is that Jesus remained in Peter's life. He didn't say, "I'm through with you, Peter!" and then walk away. Jesus not only remained, He approached Peter, not in anger or condemnation, but in forgiveness and grace to cover his actions. I'm grateful to say that Jesus has done the same for me—and He will do the same for you if you let Him. I believe that, until one has really considered the amount of love required to take on our transgressions and transform them into forgiveness and healing, grace is only a word on a page. If not for heartfelt examination of the love Christ has for us, grace is diluted to five letters and remains elusive from our grasp.

Fear of retribution and punishment keeps us from looking at and confessing our indiscretions, but Jesus responds just the opposite when we do—He holds His arms wide and calls us by name. He waits to embrace us with such love, we're able to stand in His presence—not ashamed, but redeemed. His grace and His love cover a multitude of sins (I Peter 4:8) for a multitude of people—that means you and me and everyone. He won't turn anyone away.

Will you take your stand in His grace today? Will you receive the love that is yours that He is waiting to give? No matter what you've done and no matter how long ago you did it, His forgiveness is enough to wipe your slate clean. His grace is enough to keep you on your feet and lead you toward your holy purpose. That is the true grace of God.

Father,

I can't imagine where I'd be without Your grace. It holds me together and keeps me going each and every day. I'm so grateful You came to save the world and not condemn it. Because of You, I am whole and walk worthy of the calling You have for me.

In Your blessed name. Amen.

Walk in Freedom: Part 1

Let your eyes look forward;
fix your gaze straight ahead.

PROVERBS 4:25

We as humans have so many differences: different cultures, different races, different beliefs, and different life stories. But there is one thing we all have in common, and that is regret. Just seeing the word can bring heartache, grief, pain, even anger (at ourselves) for decisions and actions we would love to do over if given the chance.

Looking back on past mistakes can be a life killer if we're not careful. It can lead to beating down and berating and reopening old wounds, which only deepens the scars. But when we're looking for a golden lesson to be learned—about ourselves, about other people, and about God—it's not only healthy, it's healing. We must confess what we've done and look back in order to find and process the lessons about what we will never do again. Once that's done, it's our cue to look forward and not look back. Ever. Only the lesson goes with us to help us on our future journey in life.

Looking forward and not looking back is hard because the painful memories resurface at any given trigger of that time or place. The weight of shame can be heavy, making it difficult to have joy in the present moment. Embarrassment can cause us to hide from the judgment of others. But Christ took all those consequences on Himself—He carries them now. And through the power and strength we have in

Him, we can walk, even run forward, in freedom from those shackles.

As long as we fix our eyes and heart and mind on Jesus, we can't look back. His presence is before us; His voice calls us to Himself and where He wants us to go—places filled with love, forgiveness, power, and healing. Our living hope lies in Christ, not in our past.

Lord,

thank You for Your healing and forgiveness for my past mistakes. Help me to see the lesson You want for me and to carry it with me now and in my future. I will fix my eyes on You, my beautiful Savior, and not look back.

In Your power I pray. Amen.

Walk in Freedom: Part 2

*I have swept away your transgressions like
a cloud, and your sins like a mist.
Return to Me, for I have redeemed you.*

ISAIAH 44:22

Lingering regrets from past mistakes can be a life killer, yet dwelling on past opportunities or God-appointed callings that we walked away from can also be haunting. Thoughts of what could have been "if only I had taken that job or gone on that mission trip or_____" can become a permanent fixture in our minds, and the conviction they bring can be deflating and difficult. Both fear and rebellion are strong forces, and it's a challenge not to let their effects recur in our minds. If Jonah were alive today, I imagine he'd be quick to agree that the agony one goes through when running from a God-calling is very real and unforgettable (see Jonah 1). Some people spend years beating themselves up over this very thing.

But God, in His wisdom and compassion, understands. His mercy is beyond measure and, best of all, He is able to redeem the "could haves" because we don't serve a "one chance" God. He is quick to forgive and create new doors and new favor for walking through them. Our job is to return to Him, receive His grace, and forgive ourselves with a renewed commitment to surrender to His will.

Our enemy is constantly working to stop us from furthering God's kingdom and walking in the freedom we have in Christ. But our God pursues us with His relentless love and uses every last detail we think is lost for our good and His glory. Every day is a new day, a new opportunity, to begin afresh and present us with the choice to walk the path He has laid before us, one step at a time. And that path always leads to Him; it always takes us to a deeper, more beautiful bond of intimacy with our Creator where nothing compares.

Father,

when the enemy calls out to me, bring Your Spirit into that place and quickly bring me back to Your presence and Your love. Thank You for new days, new beginnings, and new chances to follow You.

In You I put my trust. Amen.

He Is . . .

Who is this glorious King?
The LORD All-Powerful—He is the glorious King.
PSALM 24:10 NCV

You don't have to read the Bible very long to see that we are referred to as sheep. And if you've ever been around sheep, you develop a greater perspective of just how needy we are for everything. There doesn't even have to be trouble—there can be so much as a whiff of wind and sheep will startle. This is why we need a Shepherd to provide for our daily existence, whether we admit it or not. Thank goodness God is rich in His provision for our needs.

He is companionship when we're lonely.
He is assurance when we're insecure.
He is protection when we're under attack.
He is comfort when we grieve.
He is faithful, even when we aren't.
He is grace when we've messed up.
He is deliverance for breaking from strongholds.
He is purpose in our work, no matter our job.
He is hope in hopeless situations.
He is joy in our midst and He shares it freely.
He is redemption after we've blown it.
He is truth when surrounded by lies.
He is a friend that sticks closer than a brother or sister.

He is a father to the fatherless, a mother to the motherless.

He is the same today as He was yesterday and will be tomorrow.

He is the unexpected check to cover the unexpected expenses.

He is in control in spite of outward appearances.

He is love—pure and holy for all who want it.

He is eternal—He's not going anywhere.

He is listening every time we speak.

He is strength for the next step.

He is giver of all good gifts.

He is calm in the chaos.

He is with us.

He is Yahweh.

He is.

Let us lift up our praise to Him with our whole hearts today, because He deserves it and loves it when we do!

Father,

thank You! Thank You for Your faithfulness to meet my needs even before I know I have them. I love You and worship You and praise Your holy name for Your goodness and love.

In Jesus' great name. Amen.

Let Him In

Do not fear, for I am with you; do not be afraid,
for I am your God. I will strengthen you;
I will help you; I will hold on to you with
my righteous right hand.

ISAIAH 41:10

Going through a scary and unpredictable situation is always easier when someone is with you to hold your hand and give encouragement. Not long after my husband was diagnosed with Parkinson's, a dear neighbor who is a caregiver to her husband and mother came over often to help and encourage the two of us. Her presence helped us both as we stumbled for new bearings on our new path.

Divorce, job layoff, imprisonment, rejection, loss of a loved one—the list can get long of the number of things we will face over the course of our lives. Getting a call or note from a friend—even a stranger—who says "I am with you" or "I know you can do this" or "Just let me know how I can help" and "I love you no matter what" is a very welcome balm for relieving our pain. Even Paul expressed his gratitude for Onesiphorus, because "he often refreshed me and was not ashamed of my chains. On the contrary, when he was in Rome, he diligently searched for me and found me" (II Timothy 1:16–17). This is what's so lovely about this promise from God in Isaiah: it brings immediate relief because it's exactly what He knows we need. He is the friend and comfort we can expect when times are hard.

We may have storms to weather, but through them all, we have God's presence. We need not fear because He is watching our back. We can go on another day because we have His strength to see us through. When we don't know what to do, He does. If we can't hold on, He holds on for us, and His grip cannot be undone.

Friend, you are not alone. No matter your trial, God promises to be with you all the way. Sometimes He makes His presence known directly; other times He uses other people. One time He even brought a bird outside my window to sing a song of joy and sweetness into my day. It's just what I needed at that moment. So be watching and anticipating His nearness. And no matter what form He uses, let Him in.

Father,

thank You for all the ways You reach out with comfort and assurance in just the ways I need. Your hand has been there throughout my life, and I know it will be until my last breath. I pray for anyone needing to know You're with them. Show Yourself in just the ways they need.

In Jesus' name. Amen.

Don't Worry

*Don't worry about your life. . . . Can any of you add
one moment to his life span by worrying?*

MATTHEW 6:25, 27

If you look up the definition of worry in the dictionary,
you'll find quite a list. It begins with meanings of a physical aspect, such as "to harass by tearing or biting," and—I
like this one—"to touch or disturb something repeatedly."
I think of a bird or mouse in the claws of a domestic cat.
The cat doesn't pounce on and kill its little prey. No, it
captures and "worries" it to death. It's basically a slow form
of torture.

Further down the list are the mental definitions con-
sisting of words such as *anxiety, struggle, fret,* and *unceas-
ing difficult effort.** Even though some forms of worry are
physical and others are mental, they all result in one thing:
misery. It's the place our enemy wants to put us and keep us,
exactly like the cat with its mouse.

What about Jesus' rebuttal to worry: "Can any of you
add one moment to his life span by worrying?" Of course,
the answer is no, but the question is posed to show the
ridiculousness of worry. It accomplishes nothing. If anything, we shorten our life spans, as well as induce physical
and mental illness, which steals our quality of life. And He
wants so much more for us. He wants us to have life that is
filled with joy and peace, assurance and protection.

Jesus knows and understands that worry is a very real struggle for us all. That's because He fathoms the tactics of the dark forces we face each day. But He offers a solution, and it's one that makes worry scatter the way we do when someone yells "Fire!" and that is to fix our eyes on Him. We are to lift up our praise for all He has done. No enemy can withstand the power of Jesus, and we have His power in us—it's a promise. Let us claim that promise today and tomorrow and the next. Let us not worry but, instead, believe in the promises of His faithfulness and His love.

Father,

forgive me the times I've worried instead of worshiped.
Forgive times I've rushed to doubt
rather than instantly believe in Your goodness.
Help me remember to claim the power I have in
You and believe in the promises of Your love,
no matter what trial I face.

In Your great name I pray. Amen.

*Merriam-Webster.com

Don't measure the size of the mountain; talk to the One who can move it. Instead of carrying the world on your shoulders, talk to the One who holds the universe on His. Hope is a look away.

MAX LUCADO

Traveling Light

Training Grounds

Consider it a great joy, my brothers and sisters,
whenever you experience various trials,
because you know that the testing of your
faith produces endurance.

JAMES 1:2–3

Not long after my husband and I moved into a new community, we started having power outages. Having no power is always an inconvenience, but it's especially challenging for us because of my husband's Parkinson's disease. It's already difficult for him to walk, but shadows and dark rooms make it even more so.

I'm mostly a positive person, but I grumbled and complained each time our brightly lit living area went dark. One day, the outage lasted four hours and daylight was starting to fade—and I got particularly testy. I had candles, but they wouldn't last the rest of the evening if that were to be the case. So I got my husband settled, then drove to several stores in a nearby community that had power, and finally found some battery-operated lanterns. I bought several, along with extra batteries to have on hand.

When I got home, it was completely dark, but after inserting all the batteries, *voilà*—the lanterns worked beautifully! We could even charge our phones on them. Then, only minutes after I turned them on, the power came back on. Sigh. More grumbling . . .

Then we had a big one. A tornado came through, and power was off for three days. For many, it was a trying time. Later, several friends said they scrambled to figure out what to do for light. For us, it was a fairly smooth transition, but it was smooth only because of all the previous, smaller outages we had. I thought about all the complaining I'd done during the three-hour outages, then felt a rush of conviction. It was a clear example that God allows the minor challenges and inconveniences to build us and prepare us so we're not rocked when the major ones hit. When a really big storm whips into our lives, we're able to remain secure because we've been in training with the lesser ones.

What we see as small, pesky challenges are really signs of God's love toward us. He said we'd have trouble, but He also said He'd be with us and help. Thank goodness for His love.

Father,

forgive me the times I've complained because of daily annoyances and inconveniences. Help me to see them as Your hand at work, refining and strengthening me for the bigger trials You know will come.

In Your grace I pray. Amen.

We Will Not Be Shaken

*I keep the LORD in mind always. Because He
is at my right hand, I will not be shaken.*

PSALM 16:8 HCSB

Whenever I see the word *shaken*, I think of those beautiful snow globes you see at Christmastime. They are made for shaking, and when they are, fake snow swirls around in the liquid that's inside and gently falls to the manger scene or snowman or other Christmas display. You can shake it and shake it and the item at the bottom never moves—it remains fixed. Only the snow unsettles and swirls around.

I liken this to what happens when our faith is grounded in the Lord and His Word. Even a small amount of faith is enough to adhere us to the solid ground beneath our feet— it won't move or change. When we keep our minds fixed on God and keep our trust in Him, our outward circumstances can be wreaking havoc while our inward condition remains steadfast and quiet. And once the storm is over, we can look outside to evaluate the physical damage knowing that, no matter how bad it is, our spiritual state lies secure, oftentimes stronger than before.

It's no accident that Jesus—our Light of the world— was born during winter solstice, the darkest time of the year. His life and death shook the forces of darkness to a whole new level. But His resurrection is our stronghold—it is the anchor we have for standing forever strong. Through His

Spirit in us, we have His power and strength to endure the worst of outer conditions yet remain standing. We can claim the same words King David wrote in Psalm 16:8 and proclaimed again by Luke in Acts 2:25: We will not be shaken!

Lord,

Your Spirit is alive and powerful, and it resides in me. I want to live each day fixed on You, anchored to the promises of Your Word, and living them out in faith. You are my hope and my deliverer through all the storms I face. I trust in You and You alone.

In Jesus' great name. Amen.

Trust in God Alone

He will keep in perfect peace all those who trust in Him, whose thoughts turn often to the Lord!

ISAIAH 26:3 TLB

When we are suddenly hit with shocking news, it feels impossible not to think of anything but what's happened. We have a natural need to replay events and process them to work through our disbelief that something horrible just happened. Our complete focus turns to the event, and understandably so.

What about those who go to work on any given morning only to be laid off and escorted out the door—wait, what just happened and what will they do now? What about the tornado in the forecast that touches down and wipes out thousands of homes—what will the homeless do now? People, especially the elderly, get scammed every day of money, sometimes their entire life savings—what will they do now? How will they live? One minute life is one way, and in an instant, nothing is or will be the same again.

Disbelief, anger, grief—a flood of emotions can make a person go numb and filled with fear. It can feel as though there's nothing left, and they are the times when having a strong anchor is more important than ever. We must have hope in something we can trust and something that doesn't change—something that doesn't move—or it would be too convincing to give up. This is why the Lord wants us to put our hope in Him, not our homes or bank accounts or jobs.

Those are blessings to be enjoyed and appreciated; they enable us to live comfortably. But they also give us a false sense of security and the temptation to rely on them instead of the One who provides them. Anything other than God sits on shaky ground. He is the only firm foundation on which to place our lives and our future. He is the only One who is unmovable and secure.

When we're at the center of loss in the physical world, we have a wealth of peace, love, security, and hope in the spiritual realm that cannot be taken away—ever. Jesus and His Spirit in us gives not only hope for each day, He gives us authority—to "trample on snakes and scorpions and over all the power of the enemy" (Luke 10:19). He knew we'd have troubles, and He alone provides the way through them.

Father,

it is a daily struggle not to put my hope in things, in other people, in my job, or in my bank account. Keep me ever so mindful that You are the Bread of Life that I am to cling to, and nothing else. Help me to remember that the power You give will sustain me through any storm, and that You will not be moved.

I put my trust in You. Amen.

He Feels Your Touch

Immediately Jesus realized in Himself that power had gone out from Him. He turned around in the crowd and said, "Who touched my clothes?"

MARK 5:30

Jesus was addressing a crowd by the sea when a man named Jairus fell at His feet and pleaded for Him to heal his dying daughter. Jesus agreed to go with Jairus, and of course the crowd wanted to see the healing for themselves. The people were eager to witness a miracle—no one wanted to miss out! Excitement and anticipation filled the air as Jesus walked, and the crowd pressed in around Him so they wouldn't miss a single move. The scene reminds me of fans who rush onto a football field at the end of a game to see the players of their winning team.

While Jesus pushed through the unrelenting mob, it's a miracle in itself that He felt power leave His body and go into one person's touch. An ailing woman reached out and tapped His robe believing in her own miracle before she saw the one He was about to perform—and she was healed. She reached, and He felt it. The crowd around Him was touching Him, but this one was different. Jesus sensed and discerned the smallest wisp of faith leave Him. If I had been in Jesus' sandals, I'd be completely focused on where I was going and the people around me. I'm sure I would have missed it. But His focus wasn't on what was about to be, it was in each moment of need as it came. And it's in each moment of your need now.

When you reach for Jesus, He feels you too. In your pain and struggle, in your uphill climb out of betrayal, regret, despair, He hears every prayer and feels the longing you have for His presence. In the crowd of need around Him, He feels each prayer of faith release power from His body and flow into the believer's heart.

Lord Jesus,

I reach for You today, because I need You. You have the power to heal my heart, lead me through difficult circumstances, and protect me from harm. Thank You for wrapping Your loving arms around me.

In Your sweet name. Amen.

Safe Delivery

The one who endures to the end will be delivered.

MATTHEW 10:22 HCSB

One nice thing technology offers today is the ability to track a package. Online orders of any kind automatically send an email with a link that shows when your order is filled, when it ships from the warehouse, where it is en route to your home, and the date you can expect it to be delivered to your front door. Wouldn't it be nice to track our lives in such a way? To see on a timeline when our final delivery into our heavenly home will be and to see what route we will take before we get there? After all, this is not our home—this earth is not our final destination.

Would knowing our final delivery date into our eternal resting place change the way we live our lives? If the date were sooner rather than later, would we be more intentional to let those we love know, without a doubt, that we love them? Would we be more intentional to make the most of each day to accomplish or fulfill dreams that God has given? Would we feel more assured that, when going through a difficult valley, we will indeed come out of it because our tracking map shows that we do?

Yet this verse does just that—it says that, when we endure, we will be delivered, right into God's loving arms. We will be delivered. That is comfort to the soul and something to rejoice about. Our lives won't get lost en route, we won't be forgotten on a back shelf. We have a final destination, and God is in control of when we arrive and the way we will take before that day comes. (See Psalm 139:16.)

If you're in a valley and you don't seem to be making progress, take heart, you are moving. No, you don't have a package tracker, but the Creator of the universe has a life-tracker with your name on it. Every day, every step, we are all moving toward our eternal destination, toward Him for safe and sound delivery. It's a promise we can all hold on to.

Father,

I am so glad You are in control of my life.
I'm so grateful to know that no matter how things look now, I will be delivered straight to You in the end. I trust You to be with me on this life journey of mine, and that You will direct the steps of my path toward You.

In Jesus' name. Amen.

Hearing His Voice

What I tell you in the dark, speak in the light.
What you hear in a whisper, proclaim
on the housetops.

MATTHEW 10:27

O ne interesting thing about the human body is that if we lose our sense of sight, our sense of hearing will oftentimes become more enhanced. This brings to mind an old thriller starring Audrey Hepburn called *Wait until Dark*. She is blind and an innocent target in a criminal drug deal. She becomes suspicious and afraid for her life, and in the final drawn-out scene where the bad guy gets into her apartment and tries to kill her, she manages to disconnect the electricity so it's as dark for him as it is for her, which gives her the advantage. Because of her blindness, her sense of hearing is highly developed and trained to detect the slightest move, breath, and creak in the floor. By listening carefully, she knows where to go so the bad guy won't find her, and so she can even go on the attack.

When we are in dark times and we can't see how or where to take our next step, it's a time when listening can become our primary sense as well. With development, we can learn to recognize the enemy's moves as well as God's holy breath upon us. The Lord can be speaking to us throughout a normal day, and we can miss His voice because of all the distractions. But when our vision becomes impaired and we stop—which is what we do when we don't know what to do—we can hear Him speak and receive the encouragement and guidance we need. Would it be so far off to believe that God allows dark times in our lives so we'll do just that: be still, be quiet, and just listen for His voice? When we can't see a way, we can hear our way as Jesus says, "Follow Me" (Matthew 4:19); "I am the way" (John 14:6); "I have heard your prayer; I have seen your tears" (II Kings 20:5).

The dark can be a very difficult place—it's where the enemy lurks and "comes only to steal and kill and destroy" (John 10:10), but with Jesus guiding our every move, we will make our way back to the light and tell of His goodness.

Lord,

I am listening. I am waiting. I am willing to follow You wherever that means, because I can't see for myself the way to go. I am lost and in a dark place without Your presence and power to help.

I trust in You. Amen.

Lean Back against Jesus

*[John] leaned back against Jesus and
asked him, "Lord, who is it?"*

JOHN 13:25

Jesus and His disciples had finished their supper together
when Jesus shared a stirring He felt in His spirit: someone
was going to betray Him. He knew who the betrayer was,
but the disciples didn't and wanted to know. Without
missing a beat, John, who was reclined next to Jesus, leaned
back against Him and asked.

The thought of leaning back against Jesus brings
several things to mind. First, to lean back into someone, we
have to be very close in our relationship to them. We don't
lean on someone we don't know, but rather someone we do.
And it would have to be mutual—they would have to know
us really well in order to receive the lean as an appropriate
intimate touch.

Next, to lean back into someone takes trust that the
other person will hold your weight. You have to know they
won't move away and let you lose your balance, whether
standing or reclining. John was obviously both intimate
with and trusting of the Savior. That's because the two of
them spent so much time together. The relationship that
was built in the day-to-day proved to be a strong bond for
the troubled day that was to come. John wasn't wondering
if he could ask what everyone else wanted to, he was already

comfortable and assured that it was okay to ask Jesus anything.

This is a perfect example of what is ours when we spend time and share our lives with Jesus every day. In all seasons of life, when we wake, walk, and rest in His presence, we will have a closeness that doesn't compare. We have inside knowledge from the Savior we otherwise wouldn't have. We can live side-by-side on some days, and we can lean back against Him on others.

Jesus loves to be in our company. He loves to share about His work and His plans as much as we enjoy sharing ours with Him. He is not only a Savior, He is a friend—the closest friend we could ever have.

Jesus,
I want to be with You all the time. When I rise,
when I work, when I am out in Your creation—
I want to be with You in all places and situations. You
are my Rock and Redeemer, and thankfully,
You are my friend.

In Your great name. Amen.

Hands Held High

While Moses held up his hand, Israel prevailed, but
whenever he put his hand down, Amalek prevailed.
When Moses's hands grew heavy, [Aaron and Hur] took
a stone and put it under him, and he sat down on it.
Then [they] supported his hands, one on one side and
one on the other so that his hands remained steady
until the sun went down.

EXODUS 17:11–12

One Sunday I was in church singing and worshiping, my hands raised in wholehearted adoration for the Lord. While they were up, my mind went to this verse in Exodus. As long as Moses held up his hands, there was victory. Whenever he lowered them, the enemy grew stronger. This gives a clear picture of the power we have as long as we remain looking and reaching up to our heavenly Father. It's when we look down that we lose our momentum and the enemy gains ground.

But sometimes even stalwarts, like Moses, grow tired and need a helping hand. No one is above needing assistance. Whether a close friend or a stranger on the street, helping, supporting, and sharing one another's load is what we're called to do, as well as receive aid without shame or embarrassment. It's through our helping hands that Jesus' power is launched for His purpose.

Thinking on this, I decided to keep my hands lifted through the entire song to bring home the strength that is found when we reach for Jesus in heart and soul. We need His help, and He loves giving it. No matter how strenuous and hard the battle, He sees and He hears our worship and rushes to help and lift us up in full victory.

Father,

I am reaching for You today. No matter the depth of my concerns, I want the fullness of Your grace and the power of Your glory to shine through them.
Give me the heart and the courage to help others where it's needed. Help us all to endure together and claim victory after victory for Your glory.

Amen.

Slave or Free?

Do you not know that when you continually offer yourselves to someone to do his will, you are the slaves of the one whom you obey?

ROMANS 6:16 AMP

When the word slave is mentioned—whether in conversation, in the news, in articles—we automatically think of past slavery in our country. And lately we associate it with human trafficking, which occurs around the world. In both cases, the enslaved resisted their loss of rights. They were overcome, and they had no choice but to submit to the chains they were handed. Yet there is another kind of slavery that many people are subject to, and we go into it willingly, even nonchalantly: It's called debt. There are all kinds of debt, but the most common is that little piece of plastic that allows us to buy things when we don't have funds for payment. We don't want to delay and save for something—we want it now. Unfortunately, this can bring financial strain.

The problem is, as the verse above states, when we continually offer ourselves—that is, the monthly payment offering—to someone to do his will, we are slaves of the one whom we obey—that is, the company we've borrowed from. It literally is a form of slavery, and Jesus wants us all to be free. Romans 13:8 says, "Let no debt remain outstanding, except the continuing debt to love one another, for whoever loves others has fulfilled the law."

Millions of people are in debt, but thankfully, there are many resources available to help. When wisdom is sought and a plan is put into place, victory can be achieved. The hardest part is swallowing pride and asking for help. But as soon as we do, the ball and chain we carry feels lighter very quickly.

Debt has been around since Old Testament times; it just takes on a different form now than it did then. But this truth remains the same: the only One we can serve on a continual basis and still be free is Jesus. He's the One who was sent to "set free the oppressed" (Luke 4:18). Commit to serving Him and Him only.

Father,

forgive me the times I've given in to the enemy's lies that say I'll be happier if I buy one more thing. Help me to be content with what I have. Help me to keep my thoughts and focus on You and the abundance I already have all around.

You are so good. Amen.

Love More than Win

Honor belongs to the person who ends a dispute,
but any fool can get himself into a quarrel.

PROVERBS 20:3

Taking the verbal challenge—oh, how easy it is. All it takes is a fraction of a second, and any one of us can spew a string of hateful words without taking a breath or giving it a thought. And when we're around other people—family, coworkers, a boss, even other believers at church—we're challenged every single day. It is especially easy to "blast off" now that we have social media and text messaging. Seeing the shock or pain on a person's face from our hurtful words is often enough incentive to hold one's tongue. But technology makes it so we don't have to see or hear the damage we do. We can log off and go about business as usual with no clue as to the extent of the destruction we've caused.

I think we can all agree that it's much more difficult to end a dispute than it is to feed it. It takes discipline of the tongue and God's strength in us to stop and filter words that will resolve and heal. Sometimes the loudest thing we can say is nothing at all. When Jesus was falsely accused in front of the Sanhedrin, He didn't burst out expletives and put on a dramatic spin. He kept silent. (See Matthew 26:63.) It's difficult to display such discipline, but it is possible.

Initiating or accepting a quarrel always leads to trouble. Always. It can also lead to cut ties with people we've cared about for years, even our whole lives. Sometimes all the damage control we know to do isn't enough to repair relationships back to the way they were. There must come a point in time that we purpose to love more than we want to win. That's the way Jesus would have it, and His way is best for all of humanity.

Let us all commit to bringing honor, not just to ourselves but to God in the way we speak and the words we say. May we strive to listen more and talk less. And may grace abound through our efforts.

Father,

forgive me the times I've spoken without thinking. I want Your strength to hold my tongue and Your wisdom to pray before speaking. Please be my mouthpiece to speak words of healing, or to stay silent as Jesus did.

Thank You for Your grace. Amen.

What Now, Lord?

Glory be to God, who by His mighty power at work within us is able to do far more than we would ever dare to ask or even dream of—infinitely beyond our highest prayers, desires, thoughts, or hopes.

EPHESIANS 3:20 TLB

Everyone at some point comes to a crossroads in their life where, through circumstances beyond their control, they are at a complete standstill and they don't know what to make of it. This recently happened to a friend who has run a freelance business for years. She found herself at a point where work literally dissipated—no one was calling, no one was asking for her editorial or ghostwriting services. This is a very scary scenario when you are self-employed and have four children to provide for. Where would the money she needed come from? It was a perfect storm for panic and self-doubt.

But in spite of the temptation to fret and worry, she chose to channel her energy into prayer and to listen for what God would have her do. Was He preparing her for a new direction? She was open to the possibilities as she looked to the One who is in control, and she waited in faith.

He didn't disappoint.

Instead of writing for others, God revealed a lifelong interest of hers that had been on a back burner and put in her mind to write a book of her own. And after a month of preparation and finding an agent, her proposal quickly went to auction with six publishing houses. This is any author's dream. When publishing houses bid, it's similar to auctions you see on TV, only it's done over the phone and can be extremely intense. In the end, the highest bidder gets the book deal.

This is a beautiful story of how one seeking heart was met with an answer beyond imagination. Looking back, if not for the lull in her business, her mind would have continued to focus on the work at hand for her clients; her schedule would have been too full of deadlines; her need, willingness, and focus would not have been as great if her business had stayed in full swing. Sometimes a halt in work—or in life—and being still is what it takes to prepare our hearts and minds for God's next move. Waiting not only gives Him time to work, it gives us time to release our agenda, reflect on Him, and get ready for what He wants to do next.

Father,

my flesh says that waiting and trusting doesn't feel productive, but my spirit knows deep down it's the best thing I can do when I don't know what to do. Thank You for being such a big God and for doing far more than I could ever imagine.

You are so good. Amen.

He Redeems and Restores

Look on my suffering and deliver me . . . .
Defend my cause and redeem me; preserve
my life according to Your promise.

PSALM 119:153–154 NIV

Severing bonds is not something any of us looks forward to, but if you're married or have friends and family, chances are you've experienced the anguish that comes from the process. Whether divorce, abandonment, a broken friendship, or a willingly cut tie from unhealthy relationships, any strong connection between two people that ends in separation can be devastating. That's because, while you may no longer be with someone physically, the emotional and mental bonds go through a slow, painful process that dissolves what used to be something you loved. Dissolving something means taking that which was once connected and solid, stirring it into intense heat, and melting it so it can be poured into a new vessel with a different shape than before. And dissolving requires time. You'd think a new shape would make things better quickly, but when memories are etched and engrained in your mind, it's not easy to erase them.

Probably the hardest thing about any kind of detachment is getting through the process without becoming bitter and hard-hearted—two very strong emotions that can wreak havoc on your health and spirituality. Forgiveness is the only key to unlocking the dam that holds all that toxic waste in. Forgiving doesn't mean forgetting, but it does mean releasing the strongholds in your heart so the painful memories that try to linger have no power. Forgiveness doesn't mean the other person won't face consequences for their part of the split—it releases you from trying to stand in God's shoes and doing the job yourself. Forgiveness doesn't mean an instant abolishment of pain and scars, but each day that goes by and each prayer that is prayed is met with new hope and healing one piece at a time.

Forgiveness results in trusting that God, in His mercy and love, will redeem and restore the broken pieces of your heart. It's believing He uses all things for our good over time, because He said He would. It's a promise.

Father,

separation is so hard, yet I don't want to become hard-hearted. Please keep my heart tender and help me to forgive one day at a time. Surround me with Your love and help me to remember that, in time, You will restore what's been broken; You will fill all things with Your healing.

In Jesus' name I pray. Amen.

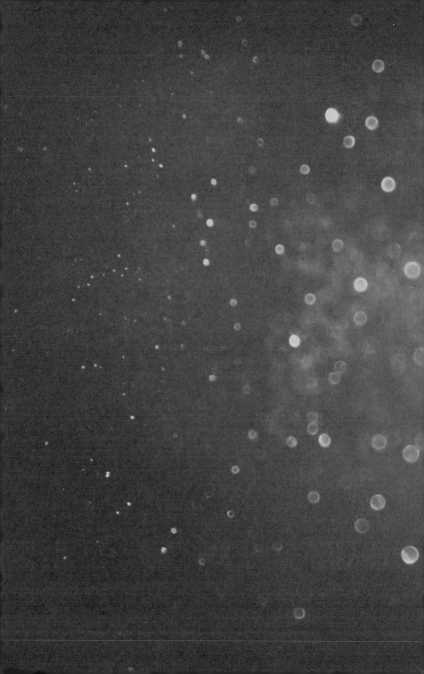

Our burdens are our wings;
on them we soar to higher
realms of grace. Without
them, we must
ever roam on plains of
undeveloped faith.

MARY BUTTERFIELD

He's Before and Behind

Your righteousness will go before you, and the
Lord's glory will be your rear guard.

Isaiah 58:8

We've all heard the term "I've got your back." Soldiers say it to each other when approaching enemy lines; parents say it when their kids are challenged; friends say it when they know we're weak and need a strong presence of courage. Anytime we're stepping into unknown territory and aren't sure what's needed to survive, someone more experienced who travels the road with us is a very strong comfort. So when God says our righteousness—His power within us— will go before us and His glory will be our rear guard, it takes comfort to a whole new level.

Not only has God traveled our roads, He's either planned them or allowed them. He is constantly leading us into new experiences. Sometimes they're adventurous, sometimes unpleasant, but they all have a common thread: they take us deeper into our calling and reveal the work of His hands in ways we've not seen before. There is faith He wants to grow, triumph He wants to display, and praise He wants to hear all the way up to His heavenly throne. But none of this will happen as long as we remain unchallenged and settled in our cushions of comfort.

When God told Abraham to pick up roots and go to Canaan, he believed in faith that God would help him and bless him and his descendants as He promised (see Genesis 12:1–4). Abraham didn't know the way, he didn't know what to expect on the journey, but he knew God, and that was enough. And even though we don't know what to expect in each season of our life journeys, God does. He is in the future waiting for us to walk in it, hoping we will draw from this promise that is ours for the claiming.

Whether you're about to step into a new situation or you're already in one, remain in confidence and stand in faith that you are not alone. He is with you—before and behind—to guard your way and reveal His glory to you and everyone who's watching.

Father,

the road ahead looks scary at times, but I look
at this promise from You and rest in the peace it gives.
Thank You for being with me, leading me,
guarding me, and loving me so abundantly.

I praise the name of Your Son. Amen.

The Way of Battle Belongs to the Lord: Part 1

Do not be afraid or discouraged because of this vast number, for the battle is not yours, but God's. . . . You do not have to fight this battle. Position yourselves, stand still, and see the salvation of the LORD.

II CHRONICLES 20:15, 17

The assembly of Judah and Jerusalem was standing before the Lord in shock and disbelief. Earlier, they had the chance to attack the enemy, but God didn't allow it. Now the enemy was on the attack against them! Adrenaline was pumping, and they gathered upon God's direction. They were ready to have a word with Him.

"Seriously, Lord?! We spared their lives and now this is how they repay us?! We are powerless compared to this mob!" (see II Chronicles 20:10–12). I imagine they were thinking, *Look at what You've gotten us into!* Yet, at the end of their meeting, all God wanted them to do was "position themselves" and "stand still." He still didn't want them to fight.

It might seem that those who didn't like conflict would find standing easier to do than not. After all, they were toast. May as well spend the last moments of life telling one another a last goodbye. But God didn't want them to scurry around yelling their final "I love you's." He wanted them to stand still—not even pace around—so it was, indeed, very difficult.

For those who tend to run toward conflict, these instructions are obviously excruciating. Every fiber of their being wants to grab a sword and lunge as fast and as hard as possible. But to stand still . . . That is a much harder discipline than letting emotions lead.

But the battles we face are not ours to fight. Yes, we still have positions to take—the way pieces of a chess game have specific squares to stand in before a game begins. But God decides when and where to move us. Sometimes our position is fasting and prayer. Sometimes it's seeking counsel or gathering forces. Sometimes it's standing in worship and praise. But the battle is His. We go where He leads and do as He instructs; the ultimate fight is in His hand.

So whatever battle you are facing, seek to know your position, then stand in it. Remember whose battle it really is, and let it be. Remember, there's a bigger picture of what God is doing and glory He wants to receive. Wait and see the salvation of the Lord.

Father,

give me the trust I need to take my position in this day with full confidence that You are with me, and that You are in control. My eyes are on You. I am waiting to see Your victory shine through.

In Jesus' great name. Amen.

The Way of Battle Belongs to the Lord: Part 2

---

*Then [Jehoshaphat] consulted with the people
and appointed some to sing for the LORD and some to
praise the splendor of His holiness. . . . The moment
they began their shouts and praises, the LORD set an
ambush against the [enemy] who came to fight
against Judah, and they were defeated.*

II CHRONICLES 20:21–22

I believe that if there were one piece missing from the armor of God, it would be the mouthpiece of praise. It is impossible to lose hope while expressing love and adoration to God, no matter what you're going through. Praise is like the helium in a heart-shaped balloon that rises over a storm to dance in the currents of joy above. Our voices of love leave no room for darkness to dwell.

Praise from a pit is a melody like no other that surely pleases our Father. Paul and Silas were bound and chained in prison, yet they prayed and sang hymns while the other prisoners listened. Can you imagine the blessing those bound men received, not only for such a sweet moment of song, but also for the miracle that followed? Shortly after the singing began, an earthquake erupted and shook everyone's chains right off their feet! (See Acts 16:25–26.) And here in II Chronicles, in the battle about to take place,

Jehoshaphat and his people obeyed God's instructions to approach enemy lines, stand in place, and sing. And so they did with gusto, and the enemy was defeated. All they had to do was sing—God did the rest.

Have you noticed that the Lord didn't act until the singing began? He didn't wait long, but He did wait. In both cases, Paul and Silas and the people of Judah all had to sing the first note, because miracles from God are always preceded by our faith in Him. Matthew 13:58 says, "[Jesus] did not do many miracles [in Nazareth] because of their unbelief." And when we don't sing, when we don't praise, one could question the level of belief that resides deep within.

Whatever you are facing, sing to the Lord. From the piles of rubble and ashes, shout out His praise. God's mercy is heralded each new morning by the robin's song. Yahweh is with you to show Himself in the center of your circumstances. Praise His holy name!

Lord,

I sing Your praise and I lift a hallelujah to You with all of my heart! You are worthy. You are righteous. You are all-powerful. And You are my God. I worship You from the mountaintop as well as the valley, because You are there.

All my praise is Yours. Amen.

We Are His Masterpiece

We are the clay, and you are the Potter.
We all are formed by Your hand.

Isaiah 64:8 nlt

One afternoon when my youngest daughter was in second grade, I waited at the bus stop to meet her and walk home together. Finally the bus pulled up and off she stepped, crying, with tears flowing down her cheeks. I rushed up to find out what was the matter, and she held out her hand. There was a small and simple vase she had obviously made, and a piece had cracked off. She held out the broken piece in her other hand and started crying again. She was upset, not so much about the crack but because she had made the vase at school as a gift for me, and now her gift was broken. The love in her heart had flowed out of her hands to make something special to give, and now it wasn't as special, at least not to her. She wanted it to be perfect.

Looking back, I can't help but think of our Creator having formed each of us so special and unique—each with our own beautiful personalities and life stories. Yet, through the battlefields of this world, our hearts get broken, our bodies get bruised, and our souls crack into pieces. But when we seek God for healing and purpose, we are as glorious as ever. He takes the defects the world sees and transforms them into beautiful masterpieces for His glory. He softens our hearts and keeps molding and shaping us into a lasting treasure He calls His own. Nothing of our lives is wasted—

no one is too far gone. We are continually being formed by His hand.

When my daughter and I got home, I proudly set the vase on my desk and smiled. To me, it was perfect, just the way it was. It was a daily reminder that, no matter how broken we are by human standards, we are a magnificent creation by God's.

Lord,

thank You for accepting me as I am, brokenness and all. Thank You for Your healing touches on my life, and for transforming what's been broken in the past into a new creation of Your love.

In Your grace and love I pray. Amen.

When You Pass through Waters

I will be with you when you pass through the waters, and when you pass through the rivers, they will not overwhelm you.

Isaiah 43:2 HCSB

Passing through waters . . . On a normal, pleasant day, this can be lovely to think about. I think of floating down a lazy river—it's both refreshing and relaxing. Usually, along the way, there's a gentle waterfall to glide under and let the coolness of the water wash over your hot head and face. The Lord is in the pleasant reliefs that bring ear-to-ear smiles.

But in a difficult challenge—when you're in up to your neck in pressure and trouble—passing through rivers means navigating swift undercurrents and rushing waterfalls that could lead to a crash landing, even drowning. All you can do is hold your breath and hang on. Is the Lord also with us in these life-altering times? Are we to think He is with us in the pleasant times and not the difficult?

When—not if—difficulties come, one has to decide whether or not to take God at His word. Will He really be with me? Yes. Is it true that I won't be overwhelmed? Yes. Can I trust that He means what He says? The answers are all yes. Rushing waters may carry us off the course we planned;

waves may splash in and over our raft; freezing water temps may take our breath away; but He is in the ride all the way until we reach calmer waters.

"What does the Scripture say? Abraham believed God, and it was credited to him for righteousness" (Romans 4:3). We can believe God, too, because He hasn't changed—He's the same God now as the One who spoke to Abraham and Isaiah and David, and so many others. He is and will be with us, but we must believe it to be true.

Father,

I believe. I believe You are with Me and hear my pleas for help and comfort and strength to endure the challenges I face. I love You and trust You to be with me every moment.

In Jesus' name. Amen.

No Condemnation in Christ

*The woman left her water jar, went into town,
and told the people, "Come, see a man who told me
everything I ever did. Could this be the Messiah?"
They left the town and made their way to Him.*

JOHN 4:28–29

A Samaritan woman meets Jesus at a well, and He initiates a conversation. He knew she'd been married five times and was now sleeping with a man she wasn't married to. He knew she wanted love and had looked for it in all the wrong places. Even by today's standards, her life was one our culture would judge and condemn, yet Jesus reached out with His words and He reached in with His love. He knew the things about her life she wanted to keep hidden, yet He met her in that very space. And her life was never the same.

This story is a wonderful comfort for any of us who are carrying shame or guilt for making unhealthy or injurious decisions—and we all have. Whether acting hastily without thinking or plowing through a self-described agenda, we all do and say things that leave a mark, not just on others but on ourselves. We can spend years keeping those parts of our life story buried deep down so no one else will ever know of them. But Jesus does. He knows. And the beauty is, He wants to unbury them and take them. He wants to lighten those burdens and replace them with Himself. His mercy and grace, love and forgiveness are all He wants to give. "There is now no condemnation for those in Christ Jesus" (Romans 8:1).

Mark 2:16–17 says, "[The Pharisees] asked [Jesus'] disciples, 'Why does He eat with tax collectors and sinners?' When Jesus heard this, He told them, 'It is not those who are well who need a doctor, but those who are sick. I didn't come to call the righteous, but sinners.'" Jesus didn't condition His love for those who were prominent and powerful and had everything together—He welcomed the humble and the hurting. He still does today. And once His healing power has its way, we are free. That's because "the Lord is the Spirit, and where the Spirit of the Lord is, there is freedom" (II Corinthians 3:17). What a wonderful gift! Let us all receive it.

Lord Jesus,

thank You for loving me before I even knew You. Thank You for loving me in spite of my sin and wayward living. Thank You for being the answer to all of my needs—before I even knew I had them. You are so faithful, and I am so blessed.

In Your sweet name. Amen.

His Way, in His Time

Call on Me in a day of trouble;
I will rescue you, and you will honor Me.

PSALM 50:15

Reading this promise—this truth—can at first be so inspiring and a relief, but then, upon more thought, it can cause one to lean back and fold his or her arms with a sigh. Why? Because, while God will rescue us when we call on Him, it's often not on our timeline or how we want to be rescued. Whether we've gotten ourselves into trouble or unfair misfortune has interrupted our life, we think and plot and plan and rethink about what we will do until we're exhausted because, in all that time, He hasn't shown Himself. Yet.

God, in His providence and wisdom, has a solution to every problem imaginable. He's got them all—nothing is too difficult. But His deliverance will be in His time and His way. It's usually a way that is far greater than we can imagine. This is because He is a "gasp maker." When He moves, His power and strength and ability are so astounding, our immediate response is to gasp in amazement. And He loves it.

Imagine Saul—who persecuted Christians—gasping when the Lord appeared as a bright light to him on the road to Damascus, then put scales on his eyes and spoke out loud. And what about the men with Saul when it happened? I imagine they gasped when they saw him, one minute spewing threats and marching to find more Christians to imprison, the next suddenly falling to the ground and becoming confused. Then what about Ananias' gasp when the Lord told him, a faithful disciple, to get up and meet "the man from Tarsus named Saul"? I can hear his amazement now: "What? Do you realize what You're telling me to do?!" (see Acts 9:1–14)

There is story after story of God's miraculous intervention where His timing and approach caught everyone off guard and His ways didn't make sense to the human mind. He wants us to be clear that He will work in His own way, in His own time, and they are both always best. In the meantime, it's our job to call on Him, to trust in Him, to wait on Him, to believe in Him. And be ready to gasp.

Father,

You are so mighty and great. I call on You now to help me in my circumstances and give me the faith to believe with all my heart and mind that You hear me, and You'll help.

I give you all honor, glory, and praise in Jesus' name. Amen.

Say "Jesus"

We do not know how to pray as we should. But the Spirit Himself speaks to God for us, even begs God for us with deep feelings that words cannot explain.

ROMANS 8:26 NCV

There are times when difficult days, challenging months, and long, dark seasons envelop us to the point we can barely think. Living one day at a time turns into functioning one minute at a time. The heart is so broken, words just don't come.

A son dies from a drug overdose; a daughter is killed in a car crash—and the mother was driving; a young grandmother dies within months of being diagnosed with a brain tumor; a husband is killed while fighting overseas. The real-life examples are endless, and the grief that accompanies cannot be measured.

But during these times when words are few, we still have a voice, and we still have a prayer. Romans 8:27 says, "He who searches our hearts knows the mind of the Spirit, because He intercedes for the saints according to the will of God." Jesus Himself draws from the depths of our hearts and intercedes, even begs, in prayer to the Father on our behalf. He doesn't use words, because there are no words to describe the sorrow He feels for us. And while some may steer clear of our circles of agony, Jesus steps in with an unmistakable touch. His presence is a balm; He is in the midst.

If this is you now, just say "Jesus," even if only under your breath. He'll be there. He will carry you. He will speak for you, comfort you, and guard you from before and behind. Let Him do what He loves to do—embrace you with His tender loving care.

Lord of compassion,
thank You for Your soothing and calming presence
when I feel broken and weak. Speak Your love into my
downcast spirit and surround me with Your loving em-
brace. Because of You, I can go on, and tomorrow will
be a new day of mercies and joy that You bring.

In Your name. Amen.

Prayer, as it comes from the saints, is but weak and languid; but when the arrow of a saint's prayer is put into the bow of Christ's intercession, it pierces the throne of grace.

THOMAS WATSON

Prayer—for Everyone

*Let everyone be subject to the governing
authorities, for there is no authority except that
which God has established. The authorities that
exist have been established by God.*

ROMANS 13:1 NIV

Given the growing heated divide between political
parties in our country, the words *troubled times* don't
come close to describing the chaos we see and hear in the
news each day. I write this with both hesitation and hope
that the presence and love of God can be brought into this
arena for a higher perspective and peaceful consideration.

As candidates from both sides of a presidential race
advertise, debate, interview, and tweet, voters on both sides
pray, rally, argue, and vote hoping their chosen candidate or
party will win. And when they don't—when the opposing
party is the victor—the effects can feel devastating. This is
because we as a people put so much hope in humans and a
government system rather than in God.

If a man or woman from the opposing side is in power,
does it mean God is no longer in control? Does it mean God
is not able to accomplish His will through them? The answer is no! God is still very much in control; He is still very
much working in ways too complicated for even the bright-
est minds to comprehend. And if we truly trust Him, we can
be more accepting of the truth that He is still sovereign, and
with that comes peace.

This is why it's vital for us to pray for whoever is in office—no matter which side they or we are on. First Timothy 2:1–2 says, "First of all . . . I urge that petitions, prayers, intercessions, and thanksgivings be made for *everyone,* for kings and all those who are in authority, so that we may lead a tranquil and quiet life in all godliness and dignity" (emphasis added). Praying for those in authority—rather than cursing them—leads to a tranquil and quiet life. Tranquility results because, when we pray, we entrust the outcome into God's hands; we acknowledge our trust in what He is doing, even when it doesn't make sense.

Presidents are mortal beings, yet we worship, defend, and promote them as gods—as *the* answer rather than God Himself. And even though they are all flawed, God can and will use any one of them to fulfill His purpose. In that we can rest. Let us pray more than we spew; let us trust God more than humans.

Father,

when thinking on those I don't like in the political arena, it doesn't take long for several names to come to mind. I humbly lift them to You and ask for Your hand to be on them. Give them wisdom for their way, and help them to be an instrument to carry out Your will for their lives and Your greater purpose. Help me to remember that You are over all, even when it doesn't make sense to me.

In Your name I pray. Amen.

When No One's Listening

"Men, I [Paul] can see that this voyage is headed toward disaster and heavy loss, not only of the cargo and the ship but also of our lives." But the centurion paid attention to the captain and the owner of the ship rather than to what Paul said.

ACTS 27:10–11

Winter was approaching, and Paul was being taken to Italy by boat. There, he would appeal to Caesar because of an accusation by the Jews for his hope in Jesus as God's Son. Paul warned the centurion guarding him that the weather would turn deadly before they made it to Crete—their preferred stopping point. Wintering where they were in Fair Havens was not ideal, but it was a better choice than to be at sea during the raging storms that were sure to come.

Paul gave a strong and logical argument to stay put, but the centurion sided with both the captain and the owner of the boat—they all wanted to keep going. Paul would prove right in the end, but he was not in control. He and the other passengers were at the mercy of those in authority, and they would all live with the consequences about to come.

Have you been there? Could you see and sense the direction you were headed was not good, but you weren't in control to change course? You pointed at the warning signs, you reasoned the best you could, you prayed and asked God to intervene, but none of it worked. You were told to stay the course.

Times like these are breeding grounds for anxiety to grow rampant. After all, God doesn't seem to be in control anymore. If He were, He would change the minds of those over us.

Or wouldn't He?

Could it be that God allows storms because in them, there are people He wants us to meet who are hungry for His love? Could it be that in the storms, He causes us to work together in ways we wouldn't have otherwise? Could it be that in difficulties, we are reminded we aren't ever as in control as we think we are? Could it be that the light of His glory shines brighter against a dark backdrop?

Instead of succumbing to anxiety, what about standing in belief that God is indeed in control, He is still good, and His plans are always filled with a greater purpose than we can comprehend?

Father,

*forgive me the times I've gotten angry with You
for not changing a course I knew would be difficult.
Help me to remember that You are always working to
increase my faith and dependence on You.*

To You be all glory. Amen.

Remember to Refresh

You protect me from trouble. You surround me with joyful shouts of deliverance.

PSALM 32:7

An out-of-state rapid response team was staying at our church to help clean up after a tornado struck our community. Sunday school classrooms were makeshift dorms where dozens of air mattresses were lined up along the walls. I joined a group of volunteers who showed up one morning to help clean their rooms while they were out so they'd return to a clean and welcoming environment. As I vacuumed in between mattresses, backpacks, shoes, and blow dryers, my eyes scanned the floor, being careful to suck up every last particle. I prayed for God's strength to be with each person who was undoubtedly tired and sore from days of strenuous labor.

Still looking down, I vacuumed toward an exit that led into another room and suddenly realized I was maneuvering around four plastic table legs. I stepped back and looked up to see what it was: a small, portable foosball game pushed up against the wall. I had been so focused on all the destruction that had occurred and praying about all the hard work everyone was doing, I couldn't help but smile that someone thought to throw a bit of fun into the mix of each day. It was a perfect reminder that, no matter how big the problem or mess, no matter how long it takes to work through a difficulty, it's important to take breaks that lighten the heart. It's easy to forget this when engulfed by problems, but it's vital to remember to step away, take a deep breath, and do something that brings joy and the light of God to your soul, even if only for a short time.

God knows the weight of our trials, but He also knows what speaks life into our hearts, and He wants us to have it. Remember to call on Him and breathe in the renewed life He has in store. Whatever you're facing, leave margin to be refreshed. Whether a few hours, a few days, or even only a few minutes, take care of you.

Father,

You are a wellspring of life; You restore my soul. Thank You for the reminder to enjoy moments that lift and renew a steadfast spirit to keep going and to keep trusting in the goodness of Your presence all around.

You are so good. Amen.

The Joy of Victory

*Let us shout for joy at Your victory and lift the
banner in the name of our God. . . . Now I know
that the LORD gives victory to His anointed;
He will answer him from His holy heaven
with mighty victories from His right hand.*

PSALM 20:5–6

Everyone loves an underdog story. You know, the ones in books, in movies, and in real-life news who are small, weak, and underestimated. But in their seeming insignificance there's a drop of momentum and drive that keeps them in their fight. And as they endure and finally break through and declare victory, uncontrollable joy erupts from everyone who's watching.

The power of joy, the power of victory, the power of winning has no equal. It's an emotion of the soul that everyone knows and wants. Could you imagine what it'd be like not to experience such a high? Not to rise up within ourselves to heights that are far removed from our day-to-dayness? Yet, if there were no trouble—no battles or valleys or struggles—we would not know the joy of triumph. Every victory is preceded by a challenge.

Without fists in a fight, a dual to match, a race to run, a mountain to climb, there would be no conquest and sense of justice that satisfies the soul. And in it all, God's grace keeps our hope alive—to take our next step, to go the next mile, to keep going at all—through the promise of the power we have through His Spirit. He renews, restores, strengthens, and inspires at the mere calling of His name. He knows our fights and He's with us in each one.

When we see others who have won, we naturally latch on to the impetus to win as well. And that's what Christ has done—He has already won. He is the finisher of our faith. "The Lord gives victory to His anointed; He will answer him from His holy heaven with mighty victories." Let us keep this promise alive in our hearts and not give up!

Lord,

no matter how tired I get, no matter how big the climb, help me to keep going and know, without a doubt, that You are with me. You are a very present help in trouble, and I am grateful. I rejoice in the victory I know is mine today!

Amen.

Who understands the thrill of seeing the first bright flowers of spring so clearly as one who has just lived through the long, hard winter?

DARLENE DEIBLER ROSE

The Hope of His Calling

I pray that the perception of your mind may be enlightened so you may know what is the hope of His calling, what are the glorious riches of His inheritance among the saints, and what is the immeasurable greatness of His power to us who believe, according to the working of His vast strength.

Ephesians 1:18–19 HCSB

When we're in a season of trouble, there's usually a time of waiting on God to come through with answers to our pleas. And during that time, it's normal to continually look at and focus on damage we or someone else has caused. Or sometimes there's destruction caused by the forces of nature and it's impossible not to see brokenness and loss all around. It's so difficult to hold on to hope that there is a bright future on the other side of the mountain of mess.

Paul understood the temptation to focus on a problem more than the provision of God during those times. He was in prison in Rome and had nothing to look at but his chains and the cell where he sat. It wasn't a hopeful situation for him, yet he didn't let his external circumstances affect the internal reality and truth that the hope of God and His immeasurably great power outshine any clouds of darkness that try to linger. It was during this time that, instead of giving in to despair, he prayed for and wrote to believers in the church in Ephesus who were facing their own challenges as new Christians. He wanted to instill the importance of holding on to the hope they were all promised through Christ.

The greatest gift we have to get through any problem is the hope of God's calling on our lives, but we have to see it and believe it in our hearts and minds for it to have any effect. His hope is not something to view from a distance, it's ours to hold and to share in the overflow of the abundance He gives.

Paul wrote this prayer to encourage the believers in his day; God wrote this prayer for each of us today to claim for ourselves until we are in eternal glory with Him. This is possible because His hope never dies—it will continually shine for as long as we need it to. Let this prayer not be shared in vain. Let us all be witnesses of His grace that keep His hope light burning, no matter what we face.

Father,

*there isn't a day that passes that I don't
need and want the hope that You give. Help me
to see the light of Your hope and to live it out
daily in the calling You have on my life.*

In Your gracious name I pray. Amen.

Why, My Soul, Are You Downcast?

Remember Your word to Your servant; You have given me hope through it. This is my comfort in my affliction: Your promise has given me life.

PSALM 119:49–50

Mental illness and depression . . . it's a topic generally avoided in the church, and I'm not sure why. Many believers in the faith suffer from it. Even pastors, church elders, leaders in Christian service suffer in silence as they pray for a myriad other illnesses that are perfectly fine to talk about. When we or someone we know is weighed down by depression, we speak in hushed tones—certainly not in a group setting or in casual exchanges the way we talk about a migraine or upset stomach.

Charles Spurgeon—one of the greatest preachers of all time—lived most of his life with depression, yet he wasn't silent about it. No, he was quite verbal and actually claimed it didn't hinder his ministry: depression, in fact, helped it. It's because of his own dark valleys he became known as "the people's preacher." Depression gave him greater empathy for what we all go through, and he became most qualified to write and preach in terms we all understand and relate to still.

He discovered eleven causes of his depression, and I believe they can be the same for us today. They are: chemical imbalance, illness, trauma, loneliness, weariness, fame, failure, weather, conviction of sin, nervousness, controversy, and criticism. Any of us would do well to work through one of these conditions, yet he suffered because of them all. I think we can agree with his words, "As to mental maladies, is any man altogether sane? Are we not all a little off the balance?'"* Thus, why do we avoid the topic?

King David's bouts with depression guided his pen when writing beautiful psalms that speak to the depths of our hearts: "Why, my soul, are you downcast? Why so disturbed within me? Put your hope in God, for I will yet praise Him, my Savior and my God" (42:5 NIV). After David's lament, he lands on the reality that, through it all, his hope remains in God—in His comfort, in His love, in His sovereignty, and in His will—as did Spurgeon. If you are one who suffers with depression, you are not alone. May you cling to the same hope that is yours when you hold on to Him.

Father,

thank You for the comfort and compassion that are mine when I am downcast. Thank You that I am not alone. Help me hold on to the hope and new mercies You give with each day. I rest in You now, in the strength and security of Your presence and compassion that are mine.

In Jesus' name. Amen.

*From The Spurgeon Center, Blog Entry, July 11, 2017

Every Day Is Demolition Day

Although we live in the flesh, we do not wage war according to the flesh, since the weapons of our warfare are not of the flesh, but are powerful through God for the demolition of strongholds.

II Corinthians 10:3–4

How would you define a stronghold in relation to your personal life? I ask because it's easy to dismiss the fact that you have God's power, even if you don't have a drug or alcohol problem. Or what about a gambling or pornography addiction—these are what strongholds are, right? But a stronghold doesn't have to be something as big as those. While these are all very real and life-destroying habits, a stronghold is anything that keeps us from experiencing complete freedom in Christ, and there are many things that keep a lot of us from doing just that.

There are the strongholds of worry, anxiety, and fear. There's shame, doubt, bitterness, pride—and they could all be at the root of what we consider the "bigger" problems. Until we really look inward and recognize those areas for ourselves, we will never be free of them. Instead, according to Paul in this verse, we will continue to "wage war" every day, which is a far cry from living in the peace that is ours when we claim the power we have through God to be healed.

Merriam-Webster's defines demolish as to "tear down; raze; smash; do away with; destroy." In other words, we have God's power to absolutely obliterate any one of the vise grips the enemy has on us. But we first must name them, confess them, and truly believe in the power we have to demolish them. How? Through confession, prayer, and claiming Scriptures such as the one given here to apply to each weakness. There are countless verses throughout God's Word that speak to all of the strongholds we encounter.

Don't waste another minute, another day, another year of life caving in to anything that prevents His rush of love and peace into your daily life. He wants us all to live in complete freedom. Let us each do our part to walk in it.

Lord,

I acknowledge that Satan is constantly looking for ways to keep me from experiencing Your peace. He knows my tender spots and weaknesses. I trust in You and claim the power I have through Your Spirit to demolish those areas today and every day.

In Your name and power, I pray. Amen.

Our Loss, His Gain

*Don't be surprised when the fiery ordeal comes
among you to test you as if something unusual were
happening to you. Instead, rejoice as you share in
the sufferings of the Christ, so that you may also
rejoice with great joy when His glory is revealed.*

I PETER 4:12–13

Doing the will of God is not easy. That's because it requires commitment to be obedient to how He wants us to live and what He wants us to do. Oftentimes His will leads us into "fiery ordeals" that are far more than we thought we bargained for. But doing the will of God means sharing in the sufferings of Jesus—and He suffered until death.

Does this mean God wants us to die in our struggles? Well . . . yes. When you have the will of your flesh—your agenda, your timeline, your comfort, your pride—battles ensue, and there can be only one winner. Chris Tiegreen put it this way: "[God] does not lead us on a walk in the park, but toward a struggle in the Garden of Gethsemane, where strong wills are subdued, and the glory of God and the welfare of others compete with our own personal plans. And we know, when we get there, that He will lead us into death."*

Our trials, our troubles, our challenges on this earth all bring us down to a form of death to ourselves, yet at the other end, on the other side of pain, loss, emptiness, and sickness, there is a beautiful transformation that brings a whole new significance and purpose to life. With it comes a far greater meaning than the life we had settled for before. It's a life that is intimately close to the Savior, and nothing compares.

Our challenges are the purging of ourselves to bring us to the glory of His presence. After Jesus died, He resurrected to the right hand of His Father's throne. We resurrect after one earthly death at a time until we are in His arms of mercy and the comfort of His love. It's where we "rejoice with great joy at the revelation of His glory." He wouldn't have it any other way.

Father,

doing Your will is hard, but of all my personal loss, it's been worth the heavenly gain I possess.
I wouldn't have it any other way.

I love You. Amen.

Walk with God by Chris Tiegreen, © 2004. Walk Thru the Bible.

Our heavenly Father never takes anything from His children unless He means to give them something better.

GEORGE MÜLLER

God Is with Us—
He Is our Peace: Part 1

*Rest in God alone, my soul, for my hope comes
from Him. He alone is my rock and my salvation,
my stronghold; I will not be shaken.*

PSALM 62:5–6

When disaster hits, life can feel like you're in a big sci-fi movie. Everything can change in a very short time, and fear can run rampant. Whether a virus spreading worldwide, a tsunami wiping out a city, an earthquake shaking entire buildings, or enemies flying into them, they are all very scary times.

Catastrophies happening right now may have a new name, but if you really think about it, history is full of plagues and disasters that have rocked our world. Lives have been lost, life savings have been wiped out, wars have erupted . . . When the reality of death and loss is brought to the forefront of our minds, the life we live in the moment takes on a whole new perspective and leads to a very important question: where is God?

And the answer is: He's right here.

God is in the calamities as much as He's in the green and lush pastures of life. He is with us yesterday since the beginning of time and will be with us until the end of time. In fact, He's the only constant there ever has been or will be.

He said we'd have troubled times, and He also said He is our hope and our future in them. That's why it's so important to stand on this promise and not be shaken by circumstances. When we cling to what this means, our flame of hope will keep burning regardless of what is happening. We can walk in daily surrender to the truth that we are not in control, and we can rest and trust in the One who is.

Father,

no matter how bad things look now or could be tomorrow, I hold on to You, my stronghold. The hope I have in You is my life raft, and I will trust You no matter where it takes me. You are my Rock, and I love You.

In Jesus' name. Amen.

God Is with Us—
He Is Our Peace: Part 2

Peace I leave with you. My peace I give to you.
I do not give to you as the world gives.
Don't let your heart be troubled or fearful.

JOHN 14:27

It's not uncommon to see frightening events around the globe. It seems impossible not to let fear take over with each episode of horror. The way some people panic and race to stock their pantries or do the opposite and flee from their homes is an obvious sign that when tragedy hits, the level of our faith or fear is quickly revealed. Our actions, our words, our prayers, our stewardship are all brought to the surface in a new light.

Jesus knew this would be the case, and it's why He gives us the best way to cope. It starts with His peace. It's not the peace we think we need by preparing, stocking, social distancing, or quarantining. His peace isn't found online or in full pantries. There's no line to wait in or face mask to wear before attaining complete comfort in His presence. It's found first by being still. It's by turning to Him with our whole hearts and acknowledging that we can't live with true calm, assurance, or confidence in any trial without Him. His peace appears in the presence of faith and belief that He is with us and He is still in control. He wants us to have His peace in abundance, because He cares.

One good thing that often comes after disaster hits is, we are not so divided. The differences that kept us apart yesterday turn into a refreshing unity of mind and spirit in us today. We are suddenly gathering and fighting together for the greater cause of everyone's good, not just our own. That's what happens when we are one with Christ—the intimacy and love we have through Him overflows onto one another. It's more the way God wants us to live every day in normal circumstances, not just in extreme situations. His peace is there for the asking—let us ask for it in abundance and let it rule in our hearts.

Lord,

I want Your peace—I need it to survive and ward off all the "what ifs" that try to rule my thoughts. You are sovereign, and You are truth. And I believe that You give peace for the asking, so I ask for it now.

In You alone I trust. Amen.

Rejoice!

I will sing of your strength and will joyfully proclaim your faithful love in the morning.

PSALM 59:16

I was fifty-five years old and bewildered. Changing vocations at that age felt like financial and personal suicide. My husband was in the advanced stages of Parkinson's, and I had no other choice than to step down from a successful corporate position to take care of him. In addition to watching my vibrant outdoorsman be taken by a neurological disease, I had also lost the identity I knew from my work for the past twenty years. I was afraid for my future and felt completely overwhelmed.

One particular morning during my quiet time, I cried out and asked God to please give me a word—anything to bring some comfort—and He did. He said, "Lisa, this is the day that I have made. I want you to rejoice and be glad in it."

I looked up to the ceiling and said through my tears, "Are You kidding?! Seriously, God?! I cannot rejoice about anything right now." Then He said it again, "This is the day that I have made. I want you to rejoice and be glad in it." It wasn't the word I wanted to hear.

I sat for a moment in silence and then said, "Okay. But I don't feel like it. I will say the words and do my best, but only out of obedience, not because I want to."

At that, I closed my Bible with an attitude and started to get up when my eye caught a glimpse of my husband's devotional—one I didn't read myself. And the Lord told me to look at that day's entry. At first, I shrugged it off—why would He want me to do that? But then He nudged me again, "Read today's entry." So I walked back to my chair, sat down, and opened the book to that day's date. At the top of the page, it said, "This is the day the LORD has made; let us rejoice and be glad in it" (Psalm 118:24).

So I began rejoicing. And no matter what you're going through, I hope you will too. I can say with full conviction that, when life feels like it's falling apart, rejoicing in the goodness of God is the quickest and greatest way to experience His peace—the peace that passes all understanding. You may not feel like it, but when you do, the Spirit of God washes over you in ways there are no words to describe. His presence is undeniable; His love is immeasurable. Those are reasons alone to rejoice in our Lord and Savior today and every day. Will you?

Father,

I love You and thank You for this day,
for this time, for Your presence, and for
Your devotion to me in all that I face.

In Jesus' name. Amen.

Acknowledge Him

I am Yahweh.

Exodus 6:2 HCSB

If there's one very clear message that rings throughout the Bible, it's the importance of acknowledging God and His Son. Time and again, especially in cases of difficulty, God wants us to acknowledge first and foremost that He is God above and beyond anything—even the insurmountable problem at hand.

A perfect example of this is when God assigned Moses to lead the Israelites out of Egypt. Tensions rose as the Israelites were being abused by Pharaoh and God seemed to have abandoned them. Our feeble logic today hasn't changed from the Israelites' thousands of years ago, who just wanted Moses' God to get on with a miracle and save them. In turn, Moses needed and wanted God's game plan, but before God would do anything, He said to Moses, "I am Yahweh." That was the first step in His game plan. Then He instructed Moses, "Tell the Israelites: I am Yahweh" (v. 6). Then after reassuring Moses of the deliverance about to come, God said once again, "You will know that I am Yahweh your God" (v. 7). Then He said it again in the very next sentence, "I am Yahweh" (v. 8).

Jesus said as much when addressing His disciples about how to live and respond as they fulfilled their commission and faced persecution in the process: "Everyone who will *acknowledge Me* before men, I will also acknowledge him before My Father in heaven. But whoever denies Me before men, I will also deny him before My Father in heaven" (Matthew 10:32–33, emphasis added). To stop and acknowledge God as Yahweh and Jesus as God's Son is the umbrella under which we are to operate—first and foremost.

I think of times when a room is filled with people talking all at once when suddenly someone puts two fingers in their mouth and whistles so loud, everyone instantly turns quiet and looks at them. In a similar way, God is saying, "Look at Me. Acknowledge who I am. Only then are you to hear my instructions and trust that I am in control."

Someone has to be in control—in charge, in command—for there to be order and efficiency, victory and success not only with each new dawn of light, but also with every dusk of darkness. He is Yahweh.

Father,

*I acknowledge that You are Yahweh. You are the great
"I am." You are above all, and I need You
for my very breath. Thank You for loving me as
You do. I am so grateful to be Your child.*

In Jesus' name. Amen.

Look for the Helpers

Do not work only for your own good.
Think of what you can do for others.

I Corinthians 10:24 NLV

Who doesn't love Mr. Rogers? His entire life was spent bringing joy, routine, encouragement, and calm to children for decades. When his name is said, the millions of us who grew up watching him smile from within. He was a true constant through generations of change.

Given our cultural and social climate, which is fast moving and widespread with fear, I reflect on a message he learned from his mother: Look for the helpers. In every pandemic, every setback, every life-spinning and cataclysmic event, there are always helpers on the sidelines. They are the ones we see picking up the pieces, cleaning up the messes, forging through the obstacles, and championing for the justice we all seek when adversity appears to rule. Looking for the helpers is not only a call to acknowledge virtue amidst the dire, but also an invitation to glean hope in what looks like a lost cause. The helpers inspire us by their actions to get up and join their efforts. Imagine what this world would look like if we all became helpers?

It's natural to want to run from pandemonium; it's understandable to want to curl up and give up when problems look too big to solve. But oftentimes the best antidote to troubled times is to go outside and help—a neighbor, the weak, anyone who can't help themselves. When we become the helpers, our eyes are taken off our own situations and onto a bigger, greater cause. And God blesses that—with the fullness of His peace and the gift of His favor.

No matter how hard we have it, let us all take the challenge to be kind, show mercy, lend a hand, and lighten the load for someone else. In the process, hold on to God's promise that "if you offer yourself to the hungry, and satisfy the afflicted one, then your light will shine in the darkness, and your night will be like noonday" (Isaiah 58:10). Let's be helpers for Christ.

Father,

give me eyes to see where I may help someone today, tomorrow, and the next. May the light of Your love shine brighter than ever through it all.

In Jesus' name. Amen.

Lord, I Want . . .

*Jesus stopped and commanded that [the blind man]
be brought to him. When he came closer,
[Jesus] asked him, "What do you want Me to do
for you?" "Lord," he said, "I want to see."*

LUKE 18:40–41

Jesus has a lot of names, and Miracle Worker is at the top of the list. Virtually everywhere He went, multitudes of people followed Him begging for a miracle—of healing, of deliverance, of truth—and He performed them, one after another. Considering He is also all-knowing, I find it interesting that in this leg of His journey through Jericho, He came upon a blind beggar and asked the man what he wanted. Doesn't it seem obvious that the man would want to see? Surely Jesus knew it's what he wanted, so why did Jesus ask him, or in essence, put him on the spot to say the words out loud in front of everyone, "I want to see!"?

Upon more reflection, how often do we keep deep-seated desires—ones that would take a miracle to accomplish—to ourselves? We might think about them, nurture them, even let them surface on the sidelines in our silent prayers, but saying the words out loud takes faith to a whole new level. It also brings to light what our relationship with Jesus would be like if He said no or not now. Would we still love Him and believe that the reason for His no is better for us than His yes? So, to avoid the pain of going down that path, we don't ask, we stay in a state of hope that someday He might . . .

Hoping is good but believing is the all-in faith He wants us to have—the way the blind man believed. Not just believing that Jesus can and will perform a miracle in our life, but also believing in Him more than His response. Jesus loves and longs to bless. He wants us to keep the dialog going every day, every moment, no matter how big or small the details or the need. So, keep talking, keep praying, keep asking. Let Him know what you want.

Lord,

sometimes I'm not really sure what I want other than to know throughout each day that You are near, and that You care. Let me not confuse my immediate desires with the deeper meaning of not being satisfied with what You've already given. Give me greater faith to be honest about the bigger dreams in my heart and have the courage to lay them at Your feet to do with what You will.

I just want You. Amen.

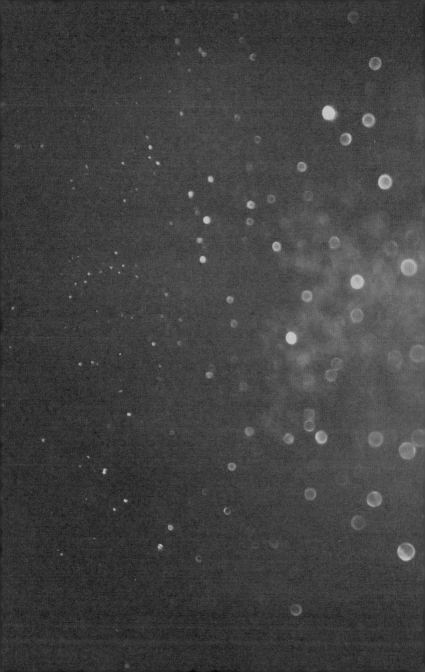

Pray the largest prayers.
You cannot think a prayer
so large that God,
in answering it, will not
wish you had made it
larger. Pray not for
crutches but for wings.

PHILLIPS BROOKS

Nothing Is Wasted

*We know that God is always at work for
the good of everyone who loves Him.*
ROMANS 8:28 CEV

Loss of any kind is difficult to process, but it's especially hard when it's loss of something we've worked so hard and long for. Whether a dream job has been terminated or a relationship we've nurtured has suddenly ended, it's natural to feel as though all that time and money and effort and heart have been wasted. The rate of return is in the negative—there's just enough strength left to pick up any remaining pieces.

When this happens, it's hard not to be discouraged and feel defeated; it's easy for fear to set in when circumstances seem unrecoverable. How will you get by? What will you do now? How can you possibly start over without the resources it would take to begin fresh? When answers to these questions don't automatically come, how can one find hope that any of it can be redeemed?

These are times to remember that immediate circumstances aren't the end result—they are only a step or a season in the overall picture of what God has for you. They are the times when God's redeeming power takes center stage and is getting ready to make a curtain call. He specializes in creating beauty from ashes, so the better question is, what oil of joy and garment of praise will He create next?

Nothing, absolutely nothing in God's economy is wasted. Jesus' death on a cross one Friday resulted in resurrection life on Sunday. What was His darkest day turned out to be our greatest gift. He destroyed the separation we had through His law and turned it into intimacy through His Spirit of grace. In His amazing love, He turns what looks hopeless on the surface into blessings for the good of our souls.

Father,

I am challenged to take my eyes off the problems around me and turn them to Your power to create something good. You are worthy of my trust, so I put it in You now—completely. I am grateful for Your love and all the ways You prove it to me.

In Your great name I pray. Amen.

A Beautiful Mourning

Blessed are those who mourn,
for they will be comforted.

MATTHEW 5:4

Mourning of any kind is the grief we feel on the inside that is being expressed on the outside that others can see. It's needed for ushering us through our grief so we don't remain in it, but it also makes us vulnerable—to a world of activity and life around us that moves so quickly, we are oftentimes passed over at a time when we are at a standstill and need to be comforted. And we all need to be comforted. God made us to be relational—we need one another, especially during difficult times. When Jesus was in Gethsemane, "He began to be sorrowful and deeply distressed. Then He said to [some of the disciples], 'My soul is swallowed up in sorrow—to the point of death. Remain here and stay awake with Me'" (Matthew 26:37–38 HCSB). Even Jesus wanted the company and support of others for what He was about to endure.

But our culture is more disconnected than ever. Technology keeps our focus on our phones and off of each other. Empathizing and comforting are actions many of us don't know how to do because, instead of looking at one another, we are self-focused. When Peter and John came upon a lame man in front of the Beautiful Gate, "they looked at him intently" (Acts 3:4 TLB). If there is one good thing to come out of tragedy—when life has been completely interrupted—we can't help but look around while we catch our breath. We see others more and know the depths of what they're going through because we're either in it ourselves or we've been on their road.

God, the Father, comforted Jesus as He endured death on a cross, and now Jesus, the Son, comforts us as we endure the heart-wrenching calamity that this world brings. When Lazarus died, "Jesus wept" upon His arrival (John 11:35). And when we become "swallowed up in sorrow," He gives us a beautiful mourning—He weeps with us. We are, indeed, blessed by His presence. He sees and He knows because His eyes are on us. "The LORD is near the brokenhearted; he saves those crushed in spirit" (Psalm 34:18).

Father,

thank You for the times You have swept in and held my heart during moments I wasn't sure it was even beating. Help me to see more of those around me who need the same touch of comfort and love, then give me the willingness and courage to give it.

In Your sweet presence I pray. Amen.

His Pleasure in Us

My righteous one will live by faith; and if he draws back, I have no pleasure in him. But we are not those who draw back and are destroyed, but those who have faith and are saved.

HEBREWS 10:38–39

A torrent in life can mean different things to different people, and how we perceive one affects how we respond to it. Some panic and run, or "draw back," as stated in this verse, because they perceive it to be impossible to get through. But when faith enters in, our perception might bring us to a halt for a moment, but we don't stay still for long. Faith is the torch that attracts the greatness of God, and with that, His pleasure and strength and "life" we need to endure.

This begs the question, what does God's pleasure in us mean? When He takes pleasure in something, what is He talking about? The words *delight* and *joy* and *gladness* come to mind. There's also the sense of satisfaction and reward and pride—the good kind that comes from seeing a job well done. The way a parent feels when their child keeps pushing through an obstacle and, in the process, discovers character and strength beyond what they thought was possible. A parent knows the gifts inside their child—and takes pleasure when a son or daughter believes in their belief in them.

When we live by faith in the One who created us and knows every fiber of our being, we are believing in His belief in us. If He didn't believe in us, He wouldn't have created us in the first place! He knows what we are capable of through His Spirit in us; He knows the paths we are on; He knows the storms we'll encounter; and He knows we are able to endure as long as we believe in His power that is in us.

So no matter what difficulty you're in, hold on to your faith and receive the rewards of pleasure and life that our Father reflects in the process. He's not only watching and rooting for you, He is with you, helping you, every step of the way.

Father,

I believe You know exactly what I am able to do when my faith in You is alive. I believe You when You say I can do all things through Your Son who is in me. I believe in the life that You give, because I've experienced it for myself—it's very real. I want with all my heart to give You pleasure.

In Jesus' name. Amen.

Above All, Love...

The end of all things is near; therefore,
be serious and disciplined for prayer.
Above all, maintain an intense love for each other.

I Peter 4:7–8 HCSB

Peter didn't mince his words when he said that the end of all things is near. None of us knows exactly when the end will be, but since the time he wrote these words—about AD 62 to 64—I'd bet that each generation of believers has felt that their time was the end. Given the earthquakes, hurricanes, tornados, and pestilence we've experienced in the last few years alone, it's hard not to think that, even if we aren't at the end of things, we're pretty close.

What's so comforting about this passage, though, is that Peter doesn't leave us to our own fearful imaginations for dealing with the end. He balances the somber with a service—we are not to lie down and suck our thumbs. We're to admit to the brevity of life and be seriously disciplined to pray—for acknowledging the greatness of God, for drawing from Him our strength and our hope, for having a steadfast willingness to do whatever we can to make a difference, and, by His grace, to love one another until that day. Peter doesn't say to first go on vacation and live it up while we can; he doesn't say to first pull our investments so we don't lose them in a crashing market; he doesn't say to first stock up our pantries to overflowing; he doesn't say to first isolate ourselves from one another. He says, above all, maintain an intense love. So, in the end, what matters most is that we love.

What does this mean for you today? What family member needs to know of your love? What neighbor would be blessed by your help? What nonprofit could use another set of hands and feet for reaching and aiding the community? What intense love do you have to share?

Today, or this season in life, might be the end of something—for you, for a neighbor, for all of humanity. May we all look and see where our love, and God's love, is a very present help above all things.

Lord,

show me one day at a time how You want me to share Your love with my family, my community, my country, and Your world. Help me to keep love first and foremost so Your goodness and Your glory shine through to the end.

By the power of Your grace. Amen.

Give His Way a Chance

"My thoughts are not your thoughts, and your ways are not my ways." This is the LORD's declaration.

ISAIAH 55:8

Not long ago I was searching for an old recipe I hadn't made in years, and in my recipe file I found it—a stapled printout several pages long. Mingled in between the pages was an old email from the young woman who sent it to me thirteen years before. We used to work together, before I relocated to another job. The email was exchanged at a time when the company, where she still worked, had just been bought by a larger company, and many of the positions would be eliminated, including hers.

Part of my message to her said that, for some, the time would be an opportunity to pursue dreams and visions that had gone unfulfilled. For others, it would be a time of bewilderment. I then began to say how terrible it was that so many people would probably have to relocate. But then quickly went on to say that the Lord stopped me in my tracks and said, "I relocated you, and look at what a blessing it's been." Ouch. He was right.

Looking back, I had not wanted to move 2400 miles to a big city where I knew no one. I went out of obedience, and it turned out to be one of the best things ever to happen in my life. I'm still here today, fifteen years later.

Hindsight makes clearer than ever that when circumstances snowball into what seem like a giant mess, they are actually ways and means to a greater end. We don't always understand why God works the way He does, but through all of His works, He is there. We need not doubt—He is with us in every step. We need not fear—He is in control. He will and He does strengthen and help us when we can't see the way. His ways are not our ways. No, they are better.

Father,

help me not to be so quick to judge the trials I face as bad. Help me to see them in a new light— a light that leads toward the working of Your hands, which is always a good thing. I want my belief in You to be whole, not just in part.

Thank You for loving me in all of Your ways. Amen.

He Sends

―――

Deep calls to deep in the roar of your waterfalls;
all your breakers and your billows have swept over me.
The LORD will send his faithful love by day;
His song will be with me in the night—
a prayer to the God of my life.

PSALM 42:7–8

A woman in my Bible study class lost her six-year-old daughter to a slow yet relentless cancer. The loss occurred years before I met her, but her grief was still very evident. Not a day went by that she didn't struggle to cope with her precious baby girl being gone. On another account, a coworker had a very good and healthy nine-month pregnancy without any problems, but when she gave birth, her daughter came out stillborn. The day before labor, she heard a strong heartbeat racing at perfect rhythm; twenty-four hours later, all was quiet. Then there was my neighbor whose senior-high son was driving home. It was raining when another car ran a stop sign and skidded into his car. The son's head hit the side window and within a short time, he slipped away. He had just graduated with a bright future ahead, and just like that, he was gone.

I've not lost a child, so I can only imagine the depth of pain and grief that seizes the soul of a parent who has. I believe it to be the most unbearable of pains to recover from. Can one even recover completely? But I do know the God of all comfort who is there for those who grieve.

When the breakers and billows of death crash down, He sends His waves of faithful love.

He sends . . . When we are overcome, He sends. He knows when we're not able to rise. He knows when the only movement we can muster is the stream of tears we push from within. He brings His love and compassion to sustain and hold us together. He sings a melody of love through the night and carries His tune into a new day, a new season of healing. Why? Because He understands—His Son died too. He knows full well the sorrow and heartbreak of a heart that stops beating. He knows, and He cares beyond measure.

Father of love,

thank You. Thank You for coming to us when we can't pick ourselves up to come to You. Thank You for not leaving us to crawl through sorrow alone and for being the hope and healing we need to keep going.

In Your beloved Son's name. Amen.

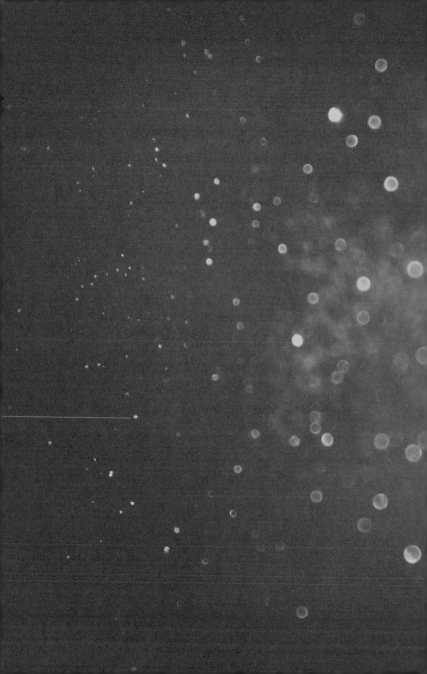

*Like the nightingale,
pour forth thy notes at
all hours. Believe that the
night is as useful as the day.*

*The dews of grace
fall heavily in the night
of sorrow. The stars of
promise shine forth
gloriously amid the
darkness of grief.*

CHARLES SPURGEON

Whom Will You Please?

*[Jesus] emptied Himself by assuming the form
of a servant, taking on the likeness of humanity.
And when He had come as a man, He humbled
Himself by becoming obedient to the point of death.*

Philippians 2:7–8

You can't please everyone. This is especially true when you're trying to find solutions to a problem that's taking a toll on your life. On one hand you think it's wise to do such-and-such, but if you do, someone will be offended. On the other hand, if you don't do what you feel led to do, someone else will be hurt. The apostle Matthew expressed as much when he wrote: "John did not come eating or drinking, and they say, 'He has a demon!' The Son of Man came eating and drinking, and they say, 'Look, a glutton and a drunkard, a friend of tax collectors and sinners!'" (Matthew 11:18–19 HCSB). Humans are fickle, and you can't please one without stirring up trouble with another.

This is why it's vital to do what we know to be from God Himself. Jesus was the perfect example of staying true in obedience to the Father, no matter what anyone thought or said—and He heard both. It's good to want peace and make peace to the best of our ability. Paul said as much in 1 Corinthians 9:22: "To the weak I became weak, in order to win the weak. I have become all things to all people, so that I may by every possible means save some." But it's most important to remain obedient to what we know God is calling us to do, and leave the consequences to Him.

These appear to be the kinds of tests that last a lifetime—they never seem to end. As soon as we work through one, another comes up. But through each one, we are only to please Someone, and that is Jesus. Our lives are not all about us, but about the One who created us to serve Him and grow His kingdom. When we remember this, His peace is our peace, and He is glorified.

Lord,

help me silence all other voices that call for my attention, and hear Yours loud and clear. Give me the courage and faith I need to do Your will and not my own. Fill me with Your peace that passes all understanding, no matter how anyone else responds.

All glory to You. Amen.

We War Not against Flesh and Blood

Be sober-minded, be alert. Your adversary the devil is prowling around like a roaring lion, looking for anyone he can devour. Resist him, firm in the faith.

I PETER 5:8–9

Feeling overwhelmed, discouraged, somewhat unsure of yourself and your future? If you're like most, and if you're honest, you are. This is because there's a war going on—a war for our souls. As Peter states in today's verse, the devil looks for anyone to devour, that is, to use up and destroy. One way he does this is by overwhelming us with adversity. Peter knew firsthand about this when Jesus said to him, "Satan has asked to sift you like wheat" (Luke 22:31). Physical, emotional, relational, and economic challenges can certainly make us feel like wheat being ground for sifting.

While the difficulties we face appear to be physical—through illness, loss, conflict—they all stem from one place: the devil and his forces of darkness. Paul confirms this in Ephesians by saying, "Our struggle is not against flesh and blood, but against the rulers, against the authorities, against the cosmic powers of this darkness, against evil, spiritual forces in the heavens" (6:12). Sounds heavy, doesn't it? Yet if we really want to address the core of our attacks, spiritual warfare is where to begin.

First, we're to remain alert to the devil's schemes so we recognize them for what they are—schemes. Next, pray as Jesus did in response to Satan's request: "But I have prayed for you [Peter] that your faith may not fail" (Luke 22:32). Next, "Be strengthened by the Lord and by His vast strength" (Ephesians 6:10). Then, "Take up the full armor of God, so that you may be able to resist . . . and take your stand" (v. 13). Finally, praise the name of Jesus. Praise is to the devil what kryptonite is to Superman. Declare a hallelujah for the greatness of God, and stand in your faith.

Lord,

it's hard to consider a dark, spiritual force coming after me—the thought actually scares me. So while I remain aware of it, I call on Your name and draw from the power I have through Your Holy Spirit to resist it and stand. I believe I can do all things through the power I have in You.

In Your Holy name. Amen.

Where Is He?

When Jesus heard [Mary's news about Lazarus],
he said, "This sickness will not end in death
but is for the glory of God."

JOHN 11:4

Mary and Martha sent word to Jesus that Mary's brother, Lazarus, was ill. Upon the news, Jesus remained calm and confirmed to His disciples that Lazarus' condition would not end in death. Then He proceeded to stay with them for another two days. But by then, Lazarus had died. In fact, by the time Jesus made it to Mary and Martha's home, Lazarus had been dead in a tomb for four days.

It would be easy to assume that Jesus didn't care what happened to Lazarus, or that Mary and Martha were agonizing with grief. It would also appear that Jesus wasn't in control and that questioning His actions was justified—just what was He thinking? But in reality, Jesus knew exactly what He was doing: waiting for conditions to be perfect so He could perform a miracle. He would raise Lazarus from the dead to the glory of God.

There are several perspectives to take from this story, but one that comes to mind is that of long-term illness and when the prayers we lift for healing bring no response. It's difficult not to question whether Jesus is listening or cares. We think, as Mary and Martha did, that He should be rushing in to stop the pain, but He doesn't respond. I've questioned Him myself regarding my husband's long battle with Parkinson's. I have friends whose loved ones suffer from Alzheimer's, brain tumors, cancer, and God didn't perform a miracle—at least not one we could see.

But in this story of Lazarus, Jesus gave a precursor to what He was about to do for us all—fulfill the words "will not end in death." Yes, our bodies will die eventually, and sometimes that process is very painful. But, He promises to do for us what He did for Lazarus. Through the miracle He performed on the cross for us, the end of our stories—the end of our lives here—is swept up in the bigger miracle He gave of eternal life. Until that time comes, He promises to be with us through our deep valleys, and I believe the deeper the valley here, the greater the resurrection we'll have on that day. He is with us, and He cares—to the point of His own death.

Lord,

thank You for the sacrifice You made so that we can have the hope of eternity residing in our hearts.

All glory to You. Amen.

Bear with One Another

Be completely humble and gentle;
be patient, bearing with one another in love.
EPHESIANS 2:2 NIV

Troubled times—especially long, drawn-out ones—can bring out thoughts and actions we didn't know we had in us. The power of fear—over the what-ifs of our lives, our futures, our families, our homes—is very real and can turn a normally calm and faith-filled person into one that's edgy, impatient, snappy, and emotional. It's easy to stand back and judge a person for their actions when fear has taken them over. In fact, we often do so without even thinking about it. But those of us on the sidelines watching are assigned to a much higher standard than that. At the very least, we are called to bear with one another. But what does that mean?

Initially, one might think "to put up with" or "tolerate" the annoying or offensive behavior until the other person has calmed down. But what it really means is to support, hold up, or sustain. In order to do that, though, one can't stand on a sideline. It requires stepping in to help while not letting yourself get carried away by the problem too, the way a pole holds up a portion of bridge while currents of water rush around it. You'd think it'd take great strength to do this, but Paul tells us the opposite: it takes humility, gentleness, and patience.

Humility creates a caring heart that's void of judgment; gentleness nurtures an approachable spirit for effective service; patience is the glue that binds them together. Once these pillars are in place, we're able to truly bear with one another—not only in love, but in understanding, in mercy, in hope, and in grace. It's the power of Jesus overcoming the power of fear in a way that pleases God and brings Him glory. No matter how bad things get, let us bear with one another through it all.

Lord,

I will be the first to confess I fall so short of bearing with others without judgment, and certainly not with patience. Please do a work in my heart to change this. Please remind me the next time I step back on a sideline that You want me to step toward someone who needs help.

I humbly ask and pray this in Your name. Amen.

Nothing is so strong

as gentleness;
nothing so gentle
as real strength.

St. Francis De Sales

Nothing Will Separate Us

Who can separate us from the love of Christ?
Can affliction or distress or persecution or
famine or nakedness or danger or sword? . . .
No, in all these things we are more than
conquerors through Him who loved us.

ROMANS 8:35, 37

How comforting to know that, no matter what challenges we face, we are not alone—Christ is with us. And because Christ won't leave us, when we trust in Him, He can't leave us. His presence and love are bound the way a parent grips their child's hand when crossing a busy street. His Spirit and protection bring the confidence He knows we need to keep going, even when we aren't sure of what we're doing or of what lies ahead. His presence is our peace.

But there's more . . . Not only is He with us, holding onto us in our problems, He enables us and equips us to be conquerors through them. It's easy to skip this truth and think that we'll be conquerors at the end of a trial. But Paul reminds us that, with Jesus in our hearts, the conquering occurs through them—in the journey. Whether a baby step or a milestone, we are able to gain the momentum we need, overcome the fear that tries to hold us back, acquire the territory that is ours, and experience insurmountable odds of victory beyond what we can imagine (see Ephesians 3:20). His presence and His love will not be removed—they both remain fastened to us with a bond so strong, no one and nothing can or will pry them apart. There might be times when we turn away and loosen our grip on Him, but He remains. Isaiah 49:16 says, "Look, I have inscribed you on the palm of My hands." The signature of our hearts is permanently written on a faithful and constant love that doesn't leave.

What trial are you in now? Or, perhaps you have more than one. Take heart that Christ is with you this very moment. He won't leave, and no other outside force will take Him away. His love and power are your blankets of protection and warmth in an often cold and dangerous world. He loves you with His life—now let this truth sink in. Let it lift you and keep you through this day and the next.

Lord,

You know the trials I'm in right now, and I am so very grateful You are with me in them. Thank You for not only Your presence, but for Your power to conquer one day at a time.

In this truth, I pray. Amen.

Why Do You Doubt?

Immediately Jesus reached out His hand,
caught hold of [Peter], and said to him,
"You of little faith, why did you doubt?"

MATTHEW 14:31

Peter was literally walking on water. He had Jesus in his sights, stepped out of his boat—that was being battered by waves—and walked on top of the water. Just the thought of this scene brings amazement! But then Peter did what most of us would have done: he took his eyes off Jesus and looked at the waves swirling around him, and he began to fall. Of course, Jesus caught his fall and helped him back into the boat, but not without a choice word that cut to the core of the problem: doubt.

Anytime we doubt, we talk ourselves out of believing something. Not long ago, someone tried to convince me to invest a few thousand dollars with the promise it could turn into a million. My response was a very familiar saying, "If it sounds too good to be true, it probably is." Sometimes, though, God's promises are so outrageous, they sound just that—too good to be true. We think, *Really? I'm forgiven after all I've done? I can do all things through Christ who gives me the strength? God will do above and beyond what I could ask or even imagine?!* Those promises sound too lofty, especially when your life is a mess, you just lost your job, or you received a positive diagnosis for cancer. It's much easier to focus on the storm rather than believe, without a doubt, that things will turn out just the way they are supposed to.

So, what's the answer to Jesus' question, "Why [do] you doubt?" He knows the answer, but He wants us to answer it for ourselves, and it's the same for us as it was for Peter: We don't believe Him. We don't trust Him. We don't feel worthy . . . Just think of the sadness this brings to His heart, especially after all He did for us—endured an agonizing death on a cross to pay the penalty for our sins. When someone literally dies for you, why wouldn't you trust in His love?

What are you doubting about God's Word? What are you not believing Him for? What body of water is He calling you to walk on with Him? Out of His love, He will catch you if you doubt and fall, but His hope is that you will look at Him in full belief . . . and walk.

Lord,

forgive me for all the times I've doubted Your ability and willingness to help me in my storms. I want to trust You more, have greater faith in Your power, and believe that You will do as You have promised—without a doubt.

In Your great name. Amen.

Who Wants to Be Blessed?

The person who trusts in the LORD, whose confidence indeed is the LORD, is blessed. He will be like a tree planted by water: it sends its roots out toward a stream, it doesn't fear when heat comes, and its foliage remains green. It will not worry in a year of drought or cease producing fruit.

JEREMIAH 17:7–8

According to the prophet Jeremiah, being rooted in the Lord means a blessed life, and who doesn't want that? It doesn't mean seasons of heat and famine won't come; it means that when they do, the sustenance we need for remaining strong to endure—even prosper—will be given in abundance. To be fortified in a season of drought means we're absent of worry, and that is entirely possible when we trust wholeheartedly in the Lord and how He is working in our lives.

Worry has a way of depleting us of strength and direction the way a pin pop in a balloon sends it whirling around until it deflates and hits the ground. But when trust is in the depth of our roots, when we are confident that God is still on the throne and in complete control, we are filled and satisfied beyond measure. God says, "I am the One who examines minds and hearts, and I will give to each of you according to your works" (Revelation 2:23). He already knows we need Him for our very life, and He sees and knows when we trust Him with it. He also says He knows our afflictions, yet we are rich (v. 9)—rich in peace, rich in His presence, rich in His provision, rich in Him— and there is nothing more satisfying to the spirit and soul than the riches of His saving grace.

What heat are you in? What places of the heart are in a drought? Will you release the trust you have in yourself to handle it, and put it in the One who loves You more than anyone? You are His joy. He delights in you. He will not fail you or let you go. He promises.

Father,

I want Your blessing—of love, of joy, of provision, of peace in my soul. I release the faith I have in myself and hold on to trust in You. Help me to stop striving in my own efforts, and, instead, fill me with Your breath of life that gives me confidence, no matter what I face.

All glory to You. Amen.

He Fills All Things

*He put everything under His feet and
appointed Him as head over everything for the
church, which is His body, the fullness of the
One who fills all things in every way.*

EPHESIANS 1:22–23 HCSB

As I began writing this devotional, I asked my managing editor to ask people in her office what they thought of when they hear the words *troubled times.* I knew that what those words meant to me wouldn't necessarily be the same for fifty other people in the same room. The list she sent the next day weighed my heart with grief as I read them one by one. It immediately took me out of my bubble of problems and opened my eyes to the vastness of hurt and pain we as humans face. Divorce, death, bankruptcy, depression, suicide, cancer, job loss, addiction . . . The list I held was two pages long, but I believe it could have been endless.

While reading through them, I began to feel over-whelmed because the reality of fixing them is impossible by human standards. We are helpless sheep who need a Shepherd. The only answer to all of them is a loving and holy God who cares. And thankfully, the God of the universe, the God who created each of us, the God who goes before and behind in each moment of our lives is our God. He's ours—to fellowship with, to call at any time, to talk to, run to, and rest in. He "fills all things in every way."

When a heart is broken, He picks up the pieces and mends them back together. When someone abandons us, He fills the abyss of pain with His healing presence. When we lose a home or a job or a spouse, He fills us with comfort and peace that only He can give. When our bank account is empty, He fills us with hope that carries us into a new level of trust. He fills all things in every way that we need. This is because, as Billy Graham said, "We are all objects of God's mighty love."

Whatever circumstances are weighing on you, let Him lift you up with the fullness of His grace. Receive the fullness of His mercy. Know without a doubt the fullness of His love. Simply call on Him and He will be there. He will fill you in every way.

Lord,

I am lost without You; I am so very grateful to call You my God and Savior and Friend. Please fill me now— fill the spaces of heartache and grief with Your presence of mercy and love. Thank You for Jesus and His living power of hope and restoration and care.

In His great name I pray. Amen.

The thing that approaches the very limits of *His power* is the very thing we as disciples of Jesus ought to *believe He will do.*

OSWALD CHAMBERS

Fight the Good Fight

Pursue righteousness, godliness, faith, love, endurance,
and gentleness. Fight the good fight of the faith.
Take hold of eternal life to which you were called
and about which you have made a good confession
in the presence of many witnesses. . . .
Keep this command without fault or failure until
the appearing of our Lord Jesus Christ.

I TIMOTHY 6:11–12, 14

The apostle Paul knew firsthand the challenges, the sufferings, the persecutions a pastor faces. He himself had endured beatings, shipwrecks, imprisonment, and more during his life of serving Christ. Certainly, there were wonderful times of miracles and conversions, but they were all at a cost he knew was worthy in the bigger picture of God. So, in spite the hardships that came, not just with being a Christian but merely living life on this earth, Paul remained optimistic and motivated to "fight the good fight of the faith."

So just how do we fight a good fight? Not with fists or a good right hook, and not in our own efforts. Human logic reduces a fight to nothing more than a battle to win and be right. Of course we want justice, but we also want it accomplished in ways that make sense to our humble minds, which we are told are like those of sheep. But Paul's instructions are to fight the good fight by pursuing righteousness and godliness. He tells us to keep pursuing our faith and to keep ourselves strong in Christ. He says to pursue love and share it with our neighbors in abundance, and . . . to pursue gentleness. Yes, pursue a gentle spirit within. This runs so contrary to how we think fighting anything should be, let alone the obstacles we find ourselves in that make life very hard.

Paul tried fighting for what he thought was right by using brute force and condemnation—until he experienced his own conversion. Once we are overcome by the Holy Spirit, we are called to a completely different definition of what it means to fight, and it's much more effective and completely life giving.

Let us all cling to these wise words from someone who knew from personal experience, as well as from Someone who knew the real weapons we'd need—not for winning any fleshly battles, but for winning souls for Christ, which is the ultimate war we are all in.

Father,

please don't let the troubles I face today get my eyes off pursuing You. Help me to be a pleasing witness through the love I have for You, and help me to have a gentleness of spirit that cannot be mistaken for anything other than Christ in me.

I pray in Your holy name. Amen.

Are You Ready?

This is the way to have eternal life—
to know You, the only true God, and Jesus Christ,
the one You sent to earth.

JOHN 17:3 NLT

"Are you ready?!" Pastor David would say at the end of each sermon on Sundays. He'd ask us all with an ear-to-ear smile laced with enormous sincerity of heart. "Do you know, without a doubt, you're going to heaven when you die? Have you finished your race on earth today to the best of your ability? None of us know when we'll take our last breath, but when it happens, are you ready for it?"

"Are you ready?" is a pointed question for us all to ask ourselves every day, not just on Sundays. The challenge in answering it is to be in such a place spiritually that we're able to say yes at any given moment without hesitation. That's because sometimes there is no time to think of the answer, let alone say it. The thought that instant, fatal accidents happen to "other people" is a dangerous denial we must all avoid. We just don't know.

Even in a drawn-out illness where death's timeline is given, it's equally important to be able to say yes today in order to absorb the gift of comfort it brings during the grueling journey ahead. Pastor David was in his early fifties and in perfect health when he was suddenly diagnosed with a rare, incurable skin cancer. He did all that was possible to fight it, but it wasn't long before he breathed his last breath.

Yet up to the end, his answer of "Yes!" rang loud and clear, and to this day, it's still ringing. His legacy lives on.

So . . . are you ready? Do you know that Jesus loves you and wants to abide in your heart? Are you sure of your salvation in Him and the gift of eternal life He gives? This is not our home; our bodies are only a temporary tent. Our true life awaits with Him who is seated at the right hand of God. Heaven is our home, sweet home. Make sure you're ready to go.

Father,

there's so much I want to do here on earth before I go home to You. But if I have only a few years, or a month, or even only a day, I am ready. I am sure of my salvation, thanks to Your Son, Jesus. I pray for those who are unsure but want to be sure. I pray they find You and receive You for themselves.

In Your grace by faith I pray. Amen.

Love Him with All Your Heart

What does the LORD your God ask of you except to fear the LORD your God by walking in all his ways, to love him, and to worship the LORD your God with all your heart and all your soul? Keep the LORD's commands and statutes I am giving you today, for your own good.

DEUTERONOMY 10:12–13

Our God is a jealous God. He loves us with abandon and has pursued each one of us with His faithful and endearing love. He is all-in with us as His children. His desire for us does not diminish or waver. And because He is so completely committed to covering us with grace upon grace, He wants the same in return. He wants us to love Him as much today as we did the first day we accepted Him into our hearts (Revelation 2:4). The outpouring of emotion and thanksgiving and love we first felt toward Him, He wants that from us every day, especially through our storms, when our need for Him is most apparent.

His love is all-encompassing. There is no height nor depth, no distance far or wide that His love doesn't call out to us. He wants us to see the beauty that lies in His divine romance in all aspects of our lives. Revelation 3:16 says it's better to be cold or hot, not lukewarm. He refers to lukewarm as being stale and stagnant (THE MESSAGE), yet He is far from that toward us. His love is fresh, and His mercies are new (Lamentations 3:22-23). He wants our faith—our belief in Him and His ability to complete His promises in our lives—to be unwavering. He wants our lives to be living testimonies that He is our God, and that we love Him with all of our hearts, all our souls, all our minds, and all our strength (Deuteronomy 6:5).

May we never be too busy, become too burdened, get so distracted, or allow ourselves to be too preoccupied to bask in the glory that is ours when we are still and know that He is God. He is our God for eternity. He is "I AM WHO I AM" (Exodus 3:14), and that will never change. Praise Him!

Yahweh,

my Lord, I ascribe to You the glory due Your name;
I worship You in the splendor of Your holiness. I love
You with all my heart, mind, soul, and strength. You
are all good, and I am grateful that You pursued me,
sacrificed Your Son for me, forgave me, and cover
me with Your grace and love every day.

To You be all glory, honor,
and praise. Amen.

The glory of God . . .
is the real
business of life.

C.S. LEWIS

LIVE YOUR FAITH

Dear Friend,

This book was prayerfully crafted with you, the reader, in mind—every word, every sentence, every page—was thoughtfully written, designed, and packaged to encourage you...right where you are this very moment. At DaySpring, our vision is to see every person experience the life-changing message of God's love. So, as we worked through rough drafts, design changes, edits and details, we prayed for you to deeply experience His unfailing love, indescribable peace, and pure joy. It is our sincere hope that through these Truth-filled pages your heart will be blessed, knowing that God cares about you—your desires and disappointments, your challenges and dreams.

He knows. He cares. He loves you unconditionally.

BLESSINGS!
THE DAYSPRING BOOK TEAM

———

Additional copies of this book and
other DaySpring titles can be purchased
at fine retailers everywhere.
Order online at dayspring.com
or
by phone at 1-877-751-4347

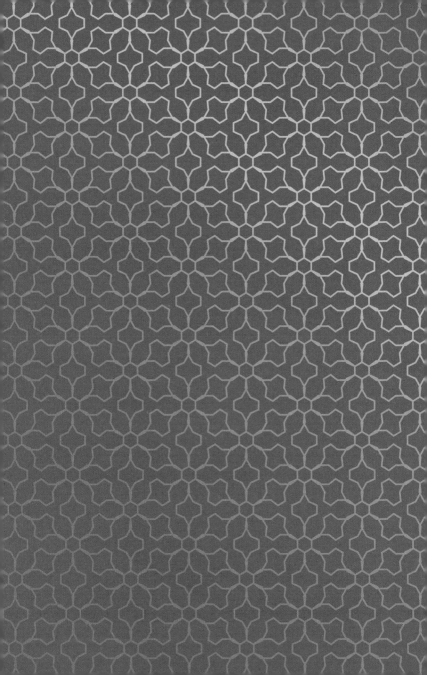